# Cambridge Elements ≡

Elements in Magic
edited by
Marion Gibson
*University of Exeter*

# THE GUT

## *A Black Atlantic Alimentary Tract*

Elizabeth Pérez
*University of California, Santa Barbara*

CAMBRIDGE
UNIVERSITY PRESS

Shaftesbury Road, Cambridge CB2 8EA, United Kingdom

One Liberty Plaza, 20th Floor, New York, NY 10006, USA

477 Williamstown Road, Port Melbourne, VIC 3207, Australia

314–321, 3rd Floor, Plot 3, Splendor Forum, Jasola District Centre, New Delhi – 110025, India

103 Penang Road, #05–06/07, Visioncrest Commercial, Singapore 238467

Cambridge University Press is part of Cambridge University Press & Assessment, a department of the University of Cambridge.

We share the University's mission to contribute to society through the pursuit of education, learning and research at the highest international levels of excellence.

www.cambridge.org
Information on this title: www.cambridge.org/9781009013475

DOI: 10.1017/9781009031530

First published 2022

*A catalogue record for this publication is available from the British Library.*

ISBN 978-1-009-01347-5 Paperback
ISSN 2732-4087 (online)
ISSN 2732-4079 (print)

# The Gut

## A Black Atlantic Alimentary Tract

Elements in Magic

DOI: 10.1017/9781009031530
First published online: December 2022

Elizabeth Pérez
*University of California, Santa Barbara*
Author for correspondence: Elizabeth Pérez, eperez@religion.ucsb.edu

**Abstract:** If the head is religion, the gut is magic. Taking up this provocation, this Element delves into the digestive system within transnational Afro-Diasporic religions such as Haitian Vodou, Brazilian Candomblé, and Cuban Lucumí (also called Santería). It draws from the ethnographic and archival record to probe the abdomen as a vital zone of sensory perception, amplified in countless divination verses, myths, rituals, and recipes for ethnomedical remedies. Provincializing the brain as only one locus of reason, it seeks to expand the notion of "mind" and expose the anti-Blackness that still prevents Black Atlantic knowledges from being accepted as such. The Element examines gut feelings, knowledge, and beings in the belly; African precedents for the Afro-Diasporic gut-brain axis; post-sacrificial offerings in racist fantasy and everyday reality; and the strong stomachs and intestinal fortitude of religious ancestors. It concludes with a reflection on kinship and the spilling of guts in kitchenspaces.

This Element also has a video abstract. www.cambridge.org/
EMGI_Perez_abstract

**Keywords:** affect, African Diaspora, embodiment, feeling, magic, race

ISBNs: 9781009013475 (PB), 9781009031530 (OC)
ISSNs: 2732-4087 (online), 2732-4079 (print)

# Contents

# 1 Introduction

## Heading to the Gut

For religion is a part of the whole of the people – a part of what comes out of their belly.

*Althea Prince (2001: 27)*

Academics spend a lot of time in their heads. Historians and anthropologists live in other people's heads too, or at least try to imagine what it might be like there. And to be a scholar or practitioner of Black Atlantic traditions – particularly of initiatory ones like Haitian Vodou and Brazilian Candomblé – is to know the head as a vessel for the gods' divine power. In Afro-Diasporic religions, the crown of the skull is the focus of forceful, recurrent ritual intervention. The word for *head* in the West African Yorùbá language, *orí*, refers to both the physical head and the sacred embodiment of one's personal destiny dwelling within it.

The West African oracular system called Ifá is not only highly cerebral but also thematizes *orí*, and Ifá's ongoing globalization has done much to promote the head as a central spiritual site.[1] According to this religious ideology, just as a person's physical head (*Orí-Òde* in Yorùbá) is unique, so too is their inner self or fate (*Orí-Inú*).[2] Not every Black Atlantic tradition shaped by these principles – directly or indirectly – regards the head in the same way, but its preeminence over the rest of the body is unquestioned (Johnson 2002; Pérez 2013b).[3]

In my first book, I concentrated on the manual labor that sustains the deities (Pérez 2016). The religious community at the heart of that study was – and remains – dedicated to the practice of Lucumí (popularly known as Santería), Espiritismo, and Palo Monte. I sought to capture the synesthetic feel of preparing sacred food and the sense that kitchen work comes to make for practitioners as it remakes their corporeal sensoria. I argued that it is in kitchenspaces that speaking about the gods and feeding them makes them real. In so doing, I pointed out that Afro-Diasporic religions, like armies, march on their stomachs (Mason 1999: 62). That is, they are mobilized by the hungers of the gods and the need to supply food to those toiling in their service. I left a good deal unsaid, however, about the stomach and indeed the entirety of the gastrointestinal tract as a privileged experiential zone, amplified in countless divination verses, proverbs, myths, rituals, and recipes for ethnomedical remedies.

---

[1] Key to this globalization has been the dissemination of Wande Abimbola's magisterial work as well as that of Rowland Abiodun and Babatunde Lawal.

[2] Rowland Abiodun (2014: 219) glosses *Orí-Inú* as "the determiner of one's lot on earth."

[3] According to Martin Holbraad (2012: 286), "Not only are references to such ideas [destiny and fate] largely absent in [Cuban] babalawos' [or Ifá diviners'] discourse, but also in Cuba adoration of *orí* (the head), which the Yoruba consider the locus of individual destiny, is not prevalent. "

What follows is an alimentary tract, a brief treatise on the gut in Black Atlantic traditions that crystallized during the transatlantic slave trade. The purpose of this book is not to dethrone the head as the king of the Afro-Diasporic religious body, but to secure acknowledgment that it is not the only place in the body where thought takes shape. Practitioners have long possessed and imparted insights about the "thinking gut" and its indispensable role in the consolidation of religious families and communities. The extensive connections between the human gut and brain feature prominently in recent immunological research on the "gut microbiome" and in the emerging field of neurogastroen-terology. Although the concept of the "thinking gut" has gained significant traction within the past decade, religious studies as a discipline has yet to grapple with this paradigm shift – with the growing consensus that the gut not only deliberates but has definite opinions (Lucas 2018; Modern 2021).

In pursuing this line of argument, I want to avoid reinscribing the mind-body dualism that has become synonymous with modern post-Reformation approaches to corporeality. In Lydia Cabrera's 1954 classic *El Monte. Igbo, finda, owo orisha, vititi nfinda*, one of her interlocutors, Bangoché (*Ibae*), declares that "the head rules the body" then tells her what happened when one day the anus, Oriolo, insisted that he was king.[4] He said that he could prove it:

> What did the Oriolo do? He closed! A day passed, two, the head felt nothing. On the fourth, the head was fine, if perhaps a little heavy, but the stomach and *funó*, the intestine, were quite uncomfortable. On the sixth day, *ilú*, the belly was hugely fat, *wó wó*. The liver – *odosú* – [was] hard as a stick and Orí began to feel bad. Very bad. *Elúgó*, fever, made its appearance … The situation worsened after the tenth day, because everything was already working badly and the head, arms, legs could not move. What entered – the laxative *guaguasí* – did not exit. The head could not rise from the floor mat to carry the body. She and all of the organs had to beg the orifice to open. He showed how important he is, even though nobody gives him any thought [*nadie lo considera*], there where he is, in the darkness and despised by all.
>
> (Cabrera [1954] 1968: 393)[5]

This story is a *patakín*, a traditional Afro-Cuban oral narrative embedded in the verses of the Ifá and Diloggún divination systems (Brown 2022). I cite it here to illustrate that practitioners of Afro-Diasporic religions have envisioned a split between mind and body, although a less extreme one than the Cartesian type.[6]

---

4  Bangoché was the priestly name of José Calazán Herrera (Sánchez 2004: 155–6). "Ibae," "praise be [to them]," is said after the name of a deceased initiate.

5  All of the translations in this Element are mine unless otherwise stated.

6  A similar joke has circulated online since at least 2004 (https://bit.ly/3MYiUED). The moral usually given is colored by class politics and corporate culture; it holds that there are no other qualifications for being a "boss" other than being an asshole. Variations on this joke are likely

For some Lucumí initiates, the head is an *orisha*, a deity, in its own right; Oriolo is not. Bangoché's tale reflects an amply corroborated understanding that the head and the digestive system cooperate and, at times, compete for dominance. They are material entities endowed with intentionality, such that the gut's maneuverings (not to say machinations) impact the head acutely. Yet in the history and anthropology of religion – as in Bangoché's tale – the entrails still lack consideration and languish in obscurity. Practitioners' insights regarding the gastroenteric manifestations of neurological disorders – and the mental health implications of problems with and in the gut – have been dismissed as mere "folk wisdom."[7]

I have now used the word "king" twice, and we cannot visit the body's "nether regions" without invoking divisions between the upper and lower body that map onto entrenched social hierarchies. The conflation of the lower body with subaltern and subordinate groups may not be universal but it is pervasively cross-cultural. In the modern era, this association has tended to rest on the hegemonic naturalization of dominant groups as equipped with superior intellectual faculties and loftier claims to rationality, which in turn grant them cultural authority and political sovereignty. The distinction between head and gut across cultures may be interpreted in terms not only of class and station but also of age, gender, race, and ethnicity. In conditions of "white supremacist capitalist patriarchy," the parts of the body judged unhygienic, closer to the ground, and prone to moral deviance are infantilized, feminized, and "Othered" as Black or brown (hooks 2000). If the head is religion, the gut is magic.

Practitioners of Black Atlantic traditions have modified these taxonomies to create their own versions – and occasionally to flip them upside down. In Lucumí, the owner of all heads is the cool, reasonable, elderly Obatalá, thought to have female manifestations (or "paths") but generally referred to as male. Accounts of the Trinidadian Orisha initiation rite and the placement of "Obatalá's stool" in some shrine compounds allude to his special relationship to the head.[8] Among Vodouisants, the head is linked to Danbala, the deity that corresponds to Obatalá, but the ceremony of *lav tèt* (sometimes glossed as a "ritual baptism") and the object called *po tèt* emphasize the head's connection to an individual's patron deity (Strongman 2013: 106). In Candomblé Nagô and Ketu, the Brazilian Oxalá governs the head, along with the primordial female

---

older than Bangoché's *patakín* (www.elesquiudense.com.ar/notas.php?id_nota=94538, www .chispaisas.info/moralejas2.htm; from February 12, 2009).

[7] www.medlink.com/articles/neurogastroenterology.

[8] The ceremony of *desonay/desayanne/desien/désonu* is analogous to the Lucumí *kariocha* (Castor 2017; Houk 1995).

*orixá* Iemanjá (Daniel 2005: 75; Forde 2018: 27n27). Saramaka, Ndyuka, Kumina, Komfa, and Shango traditions, among others, identify the head as the physical container in which guardian spirits reside, and these are always senior and "higher" relative to the devotee (Herskovits and Herskovits 1934: 153, 227; Platvoet 1982: 123; Price 2007).

In several of these traditions, the gut belongs to certain less elevated, more down-to-earth and subversive deities, like the mischievous path opener (and closer) Eleggúa. In due course, I tackle these anatomical cum cosmological relationships. But such correlations leave many questions unresolved about the gut's place in religious practice. Black Atlantic "embodied physiology," story-telling, and ceremonies that thematize the gut have emphasized the gut's ability to act decisively and produce knowledge (Daniel 2005: 74). The gut's vulner-ability to magic and sorcery, particularly through the ingestion of noxious substances, has given rise to a rich pharmacopeia. Indeed, among the chief undertakings of Afro-Diasporic healers and diviners has been the alleviation of suffering caused by the stomach and intestines. Their ministrations have impli-cated patients in the world of the gods and ancestors, leading not infrequently to their clients' transformation into religious subjects. As practitioners, they have discovered that, to serve the spirits, they must occasionally – and sometimes permanently – surrender control over their guts. Even today, devotees are obliged to consume special foods in rites of passage and consent to the impos-ition of food taboos that may be lifelong.

The gut is experienced in perhaps the most intense and memorable way through sensations suddenly perceived within it, and practitioners of Afro-Diasporic religions have historically singled out abdominal aches, pains, and twinges as messages from the gods and ancestors. The murk of the gut conduces to the play of concealment and revelation that characterizes Black Atlantic symbolism and ritualization. To grasp the significance of gut feelings, instincts, and reactions, it is necessary to probe into their discursive construction (as common idioms that may not index actual sensations at all) as well as their tangible materiality. Sometimes people say they feel something in their gut because they do; at other times they cite gut feelings in the absence of somatic stimuli as verbal shorthand for hunches and sentiments that should not – or cannot – be ignored.

What can be gleaned about the gut from the speech genres in which it appears? For some compelling answers, we might look to affect theory. But despite its conceptual and methodological sophistication, the contemporary scholarship on affect and emotion tends to dichotomize mind and body – brain and belly – to a greater extent than Afro-Diasporic religions do. In this corpus as in everyday parlance, the gut is synecdochic of the body and the really real, an undeniable quantum vibrating with untold potentiality that no representation can fully capture (Mazzarella 2009: 299). I nevertheless take abundant inspiration from Sara Ahmed's ([2004] 2014) trenchant exploration of the "stickiness" of feeling, along with other scholars attentive to sentiment and sensation in the formation of subjectivities.

## Gut Check

GUTs [Grand Unified Theories that sought to unite the strong, weak, and electromagnetic quanta in a sympathetic symmetry that would include gravity and overturn the bolt-it-together-somehow methods of The Standard Model] had their heart in the right place; they wanted to recognise the true relationship between the three fundamental forces. Now, more than ever, crossing into the twenty-first century, our place in the universe and the place of the universe in us, is proving to be one of active relationship.

*Jeanette Winterson (1997: 99)*

What is the gut in this book? Colloquially, the guts are the human body's soft innermost insides: the stomach and the small and large intestines. I take my cue from Black Canadian novelist and essayist Althea Price (2001: 27):

"The belly" I use to refer to the place where emotions are held, the stomach, the center of the body. (When a Caribbean woman really bawls, she does so holding her belly and saying, "Ooi, me belly! Me belly!") I speak of the belly also as the understanding of it as a place where nourishment is processed, the place where food is digested, stored, and then dispersed to the rest of the body.

Technically, the gut also comprises the mouth, esophagus, rectum, and anus, but these digestive cavities and passageways figure less conspicuously in the present Element. The slang phrase "getting in someone's guts" means "having penetrative sex with," but genitals and reproductive organs are beyond the scope of my study.[9] Within its purview are the singular and plural forms of gut in sundry gradations of meaning.

I offer no Grand Unified Theory of the gut or guts in Black Atlantic traditions. While my method is comparative, I specialize in the study of Lucumí and the lion's share of my examples are drawn from Afro-Cuban religious formations. Sections 2 and 3 examine gut feelings and the beings that reside in the belly. Section 4 considers possible West and Central African precedents for the Afro-Diasporic "gut-brain axis" (Bruce and Lane Ritchie 2018). Section 5 discusses the offering of guts to gods and ancestors as the object of racist fantasy and

---

[9] I regret not being able to tease out the gut's relationship to sexuality in this Element. "Gut politics" is profoundly gendered, as in its presumption that cisgender women and homosexual men do not have the "guts" of heterosexual cisgender men (Babatunde 1992: 92–3; Carden-Coyne 2005; LeBlanc 2010: 169).

ordinary material reality. Sections 6 and 7 establish that the stomach and intestines figure in ritual practice and the collective historical memory of religious ancestors. Section 8 connects the literal gutting that transpires in kitchenspaces to the figurative spilling of guts that accompanies it. Combining participant observation and archival research, *The Gut* gestures tentatively toward the "active relationship" mentioned in the passage from Jeanette Winterson's novel *Gut Symmetries*, as expressed in Afro-Diasporic religions.

My aspirations are modest, to the point that it might be prudent to urge my reader against looking in these pages for [E]nlightenment. This master trope, reliant on the symbolism of knowledge as light and ignorance as darkness, gave its name to a philosophical movement that ascended to ideological supremacy on the backs of enslaved peoples. Their becoming Black led to the birth of whiteness as a category and condition (in the sense of stipulation) for selfhood and citizenship (Derrida and Moore 1974; Hornback 2019).

As Black feminist scholars like Cynthia B. Dillard (2000) have established, the racialized and gendered visual metaphors we use to convey our findings have the ability to shape their reception quite apart from our best intentions. Without adopting an "endarkened feminist epistemology," I have been sensitized to the ways that terms like *clarify* and *illuminate* not only continue to uphold the negative connotations of darkness (and, by extension, Blackness) but also reinforce the overwhelming ocularcentrism of scholarly discourses.

I ask my reader to sit with the discomfort caused by the unaccustomed tack taken here. In keeping with my argument, I lean into an interdisciplinary analysis of the gut that prioritizes haptics, tactility, and the unnerving "interoceptive sensations" felt deep within the abdomen (Machon 2009; Stroeken 2008: 468). Since these perceptions are at times so complex as to be unverbalizeable, I strive for precision in the portrayal of gut phenomena as a means of advancing scholarly debates on embodiment, emotion, and cognition in religious studies. By concentrating on Afro-Diasporic examples in their circumstantial particularity, I hope to uncover historical patterns and enable what Jonathan Z. Smith (1990: 53) dubbed the "magic" of serious cross-cultural comparison, "an active, at times even playful enterprise of deconstruction and reconstruction" that has the power to redescribe the world, thereby changing it.

Throughout I touch on themes currently under investigation in the cognitive science of religion, in the interest of providing a non-Euro-American model of "mind" that locates it as one coordinate on the gut-brain axis. In doing so, I do not simply seek representation for people of African descent routinely excluded from theorization of "human nature" or "the body," in a rhetorical move analogous to the institutional diversity, equity, and inclusion work some of us are called to do within our colleges and universities (Ahmed 2012). Defining the Afro-Diasporic "thinking gut" as one more "local theory of mind" is not sufficient to decolonize disciplinary formations organized by "settler colonial logics" and informed by evolutionary, behavioral, and developmental psychology (Avalos 2018, 2020; Lloyd and Wolfe 2015; Luhrmann 2014; Taves 2014). Moreover, the attainment of nuanced, nontokenizing representation is no simple task. Lucien Lévy-Bruhl's *La mentalité primitive* (1922) also aspired to correct the logocentric record with its speculation on the prelogical thought and "mystical participation" of "savages."

To open up the gut in Black Atlantic traditions now is to broach a sensitive subject in gut-wrenching times. To be "gutted" means to be in mourning, doubled over in grief and sick to our stomachs. Physiologically, we can say why this is so, from the vagaries of the vagus nerve, to the reflux that accompanies the extinction of gut flora by antibiotics. There is a political dimension to this pain, however. To encapsulate what is happening to hard-won civil rights and environmental protections in the United States, commentators often reach for the term "gutted." The term "politics of the belly" was coined in the context of West African experience, but it well applies to the eviscerating violence of the Afro-Diasporic present (Bayart 1989). The knots in our stomachs sound the alarm of intersubjective and social emergency. An inquiry like *The Gut* risks heaping insult onto injury and exposing practitioners for the nth time to the glare of unscrupulous anti-Black scrutiny.

With this very real danger comes the outside chance that we might be able to realize the gut's outsized role in Afro-Diasporic religious thought. *The Gut* commits to relativizing – or, better yet, provincializing – the brain as the sole locus of reason, as per secular-liberal political frameworks for thought and agency (Chakrabarty 2000). What we stand to gain from broadening the category of "cognitive" along these lines is akin to the recognition that distinguishing between black (and/or Black) magic and religion has little heuristic value, but in practice has served to justify the marginalization of stigmatized and minoritized groups (Chireau 1993). As Diana Paton (2009: 2) writes, "the concept [of] 'religion' has acted as a race-making category: a marker of the line between supposedly 'civilized' peoples (who practice religion) and 'primitive' peoples (who practice superstition or magic)." The expansion of "mind" promises to recast Afro-Diasporic religions as more than bottomless wells of magic spells and inspiration for pop-culture appropriation. Expanding "mind" to incorporate the gut may assist us in coming to grips with the anti-Blackness that has prevented Black Atlantic knowledges from being accepted as such.

Accordingly, this Element owes less to Rabelais (1854: 257) – *"Et tout pour la trippe!"* – than it does to Bangoché. Like the alimentary tract in his story, a book is a dense bundle of fibers, a conduit for both gross matter and subtleties. Only after it closes does its power become plain.

## 2 Gut Feelings

Deep folklore is a riff, a refrain, a gut feeling and a gut reaction, a theory of sensing and sensation, of movement across space and through time.

*Kay Turner (2021: 10)*

Within the past decade, scientific research on the gut has challenged assumptions about moral-ethical decision-making, consciousness, and volition. In biology and the emerging field of neurogastroenterology, discoveries about the gut as a "second brain" and site of embodied cognition have led to a surge in the publication of journals and monographs to disseminate the latest findings. The growing acknowledgment of the "enteric brain" in the 1990s coincided with (but does not seem to have influenced) the "sensory turn" in the social sciences and humanities. The motto for this turn could be summed up as "the body knows." It succeeded in redirecting scholars in religious studies toward the study of affective states, corporeal knowledge, and the "stuff" (objects, spaces, and media) of everyday ritual practice.

Contrary to the impression generated by debates over the value of the liberal arts, the hard sciences have been playing catch-up to these developments. In June 2021, the journal *Nature* reported on an article in which the authors asked, "has the increasingly recognized impact of affective phenomena ushered in a new era, the era of affectivism?" (Dukes et al., 2021). For anyone acquainted with the "affective turn" and the emergence of affect theory in the early 2000s, the question would seem oblivious at best.

Some insights concerning the enteric nervous system and alimentary canal in particular have since been pursued in isolated studies by scholars interested in the potential of cognitive science for illuminating religious experience. These insights have yet to be addressed within the context of a particular set of religious formations. I say "addressed" and not "applied" because this Element exists in part to recognize Black Atlantic knowledges, which should not be reduced to raw material for theory but acknowledged as the product of theorization (Wiredu 2004).

Asserting that these knowledges are knowable leaves me open to charges of reification, bearing in mind the intricacies involved in stitching together disparate accounts of "inescapably historical entanglements of matter, praxis, and language" experienced by generations of different practitioners into something resembling a corpus of "deep folklore" (Palmié 2018: 805). Anthropologist Rane Willerslev's critique of the term "worldview" and studies predicated on it might be apposite here; for Willerslev (2007: 156), worldview implies "that a body of context-free, propositional knowledge about spiritual beings, their characteristics and interrelations, lies fully formed inside people's heads."

Although greater contextualization of the knowledges attested here would be optimal, I should explain that propositional knowledge is not a core component of them. Formal propositions of the sort practitioners "believe in" are few and far between, as Afro-Diasporic religions do not have creeds. They are orthopraxic rather than orthodoxic – that is, they focus on correct actions in everyday conduct and ritual over proper thought and belief(s). Personal knowledge and procedural "knowledge *how*" to do things with skill – to felicitous effect – has taken precedence in these traditions over propositional "knowledge *that*" something is true based on empirical facts (Carr 2003: 20).[10] While my invocation of "knowledges" in these pages might arouse the same skepticism "worldview" does, I nevertheless stand with scholars whose studies have documented "embodied knowledge(s)" of myriad types within the Black Atlantic world. In groping toward an appreciation of the gut as the basis for religious knowledge, I rely on practitioners' words, in addition to historical and ethnographic documentation, to ascertain what they can plausibly be said to have known. As we will see, their conceptualizations of the gut have not been – and are not – "purely" anatomical, but incorporate feeling and possess cognitive dimensions that in previous epochs would have been written off as unscientific, magical, and/or inherently religious.

## Trusting Your Gut

The phrase "gut feelings" is used so often in English, it is hard to pin down what people mean by it. When people announce that they are "operating from the gut" – say, on social media – the statement is meant to inaugurate a new phase of personal integrity and candor. They are declaring that, from now on, they are doing only what feels right. Tweets and memes exhort readers to "pay attention to your gut" or "listen to your gut," as if these phrases point to self-evident and universal sensations. When queried, people state that gut feelings feel sharp (but not razor-sharp), peculiar, prickly, nebulous, like a menstrual cramp, like the onset of flatulence, a dull poke in the side, or percussive taps (Flora 2007). Survivors of violence and those who suffer from chronic anxiety report difficulty in separating gut feelings from physiological responses like a "nervous stomach" (or an uncanny sense of impending doom). The dread that one is about to lose control of one's bowels or succumb to illness may be traces of traumatic

---

[10] Procedural knowledge does entail some propositional knowledge, but it is not at the fore in this epistemological category.

bodily memory. Recent studies have outlined the role that neurotransmitters and gut flora play in producing these feelings, although they do not fully explain them.

Gut feelings do not always translate into other languages, even to those historically spoken by practitioners of Black Atlantic traditions in the Caribbean and Latin America. The Dutch *gut reactie* and *buikgevoel* ("gut reaction" and "gut feeling," respectively) are the closest to the English denotatively; *onderbuikgevoel* ("underbelly feeling") carries the negative connotation of prejudicial judgment. The Spanish for "gut instinct" is *presentimiento* or *instinto visceral*, both of which insinuate a premonition of future events akin to a "sixth sense." The closest term with a somatic compo-nent would be *corazonada*, a hunch or impulse that originates in or fills the heart. In French, *avoir du cran* means to have the guts (in the sense of courage) to do something, but "gut feeling" is rendered as *pressentiment, intuition*, or *instinct*, with much the same connotations as their English cognates. The Portuguese for "gut feeling" is *pressentimento;* "guts," as a synonym for courage, is *fígado* (liver) or *estômago* (stomach). In Haitian Kreyòl, the words *grenn, kran, zantray*, and *zenba* refer to the entrails, insides, or vitals, but – like *heart* in English – they also connote bravery and determination. Relatedly, *grenn* and *zantray* mean close or intimate friend.[11] In both French and Kreyòl, *estomaqué* (or *estomake*) means to take offense, to be scandalized by something, or "[t]o be angry because of injured pride, because your feelings have been hurt" (Targète and Urciolo 1993: 62).

Given the substantial volume of scholarship on religion, emotion, and senti-ment, the analysis of gut feelings as a component of religious experience has a surprisingly recent history. As often as they feature in first-person and ethno-graphic accounts, they have not been the object of sustained inquiry within religious studies. In the anthropology of religion, gut feelings have been interpreted primarily as facilitating the conversion process by registering assent to particular messages and legitimating the authority of religious leaders (Lohmann 2003). For one practitioner in a study of conversion to Christian Spiritualism, "the interactions with [a] medium 'helped explain things to me in ways consistent with my gut feelings' in ways that the 'Christian spiel' never had" (Brown 2003: 141). Similarly, most theological and philosophical

---

[11] *Zantray* means guts and is "an acronym for Zanfan Tradisyon Ayisyen (Children of the Haitian Tradition), an organization for the defense of the Vodou religion ... formed because of the lynchings of Vodou priests after the departure of President Jean-Claude Duvalier in 1986" (Hebblethwaite 2012: 302). The usage of *zantray* in this context recalls the adoption of GUTS as an acronym for Gay Urban Truth Squad (sometimes jokingly referred to as the Gay Urban Terrorist Squad), a Dallas activist group founded in 1987.

investigations of gut feelings have dealt with them as a factor in the formulation of ethical judgments (Wisneski, Lytle, and Skitka 2009).

Some scholars deem gut feelings to be a decision-making resource superior to imaginative reflection or intellectual calculation. They proceed as if "gut reactions constitute a more authentic moral response than some internal struggle to adhere to a higher, absolute external standard" (Hoffman 1992: 221). Others view such reactions as a lower form of moral assessment, an "irrational impulse" that contributes to the entrenchment of biases (Stannard 1982: 75). "Gut reactions and prejudices" occupy the same (il)logical status, as if gut feelings were the corporeal corollary of mental preconceptions or a species of "cognitive shortcut" (Browse 2018: 62).

Gut feelings have figured with greater reference to actual physical sensation in ethnographies of indigenous peoples and their constructions of kinship (Viveiros de Castro 2009). These studies have scrutinized sensations analogous to gut feelings – how and why certain guts can be said to feel – as well as their import within discourses of intimacy and genealogy (Povinelli 2006: 85). While these studies have stopped short of considering the rhetorical citation of gut feelings as a type of speech genre – one arguably aimed at ex post rationalization – they have devised strategies for contextualizing interlocutors' utterances (Redmond 2008). These studies have not tended to thematize religion, however, but rather used gut feelings to underwrite the concept of culture, especially as an index of its material – specifically somatic – reality. For example, Anita von Poser (2013: 213) analyzes foodways as generating empathy (among other feelings that engender "relatedness") and mentions cooking as one aspect of "food-related socialization" that promotes durable configurations of personhood in Bosmun, Papua New Guinea.

Perhaps the most intriguing such study is Roger Ivar Lohmann's account of the Papuan Asabano people and their acceptance of Baptist Christianity as their primary religious affiliation in the late twentieth century. Lohmann (2003: 110) explored the phenomenon of "abdominally-residing volition, common in Melanesia," such that, "For [the Asabano], cognition takes place 'in the belly,' and the conversion process involves 'turning the belly' to house and be animated by a universal Holy Spirit" (Austin-Broos 2003: 4). Lohmann (2011: 110) later revised his argument, noting that an interview with a missionary had led him to overstate the gut's cognitive function and conceding that his "general Asabano model of souls as living in the intestines was not widely shared." Lohmann (2011: 101) came to the conclusion that, despite the younger Asabanos' exposure to Western styles of schooling that situate thought within the human brain, "the heart remains the primary locus of mentation [thinking, feeling, imagining, and planning]." Nevertheless, Lohmann's research points to the importance of conceiving of cognition beyond the head. His revision of his prior statements has special relevance for us here because it indicates the need to define the gut expansively beyond the alimentary tract, in accordance with local understandings.

Complicating any analysis of "gut feelings" is the fact that scholars in myriad disciplines tend to take their occurrence as reported by research subjects at face value, without distinguishing whether the phrase "gut feelings" is employed as an idiomatic expression or designates an identifiable sensation, like a tightening of the stomach muscles (Liyanage 2016: 22–33; Prinz 2004). Douglas Robinson (2013: 222) draws attention to the gut as a metonym in his definition of "somatic response":

> the felt phenomenology of somatic marking; referred to colloquially in terms of the "gut" ("gut reaction," "gut feeling," "gut instinct," "gut check," "go with your gut," "know something in your gut"), a synecdochic use of the enteric nervous system to represent the entire autonomic nervous system.

Attributed to neuroscientist Antonio Damasio, the theory of "somatic markers" has shaped research on gut feelings at the intersections of philosophy, medical anthropology, and cognitive science. Mark R. Wynn (2005: 116) explains,

> A somatic marker is a visceral or non-visceral feeling that marks out an option as bad (or, less importantly, as good) independently of any discursively articulated assessment of the option. More colloquially we could talk of registering the character of an option in a "gut feeling." It is because of our gut feelings that we do not get lost in the kind of indefinitely extended examination of possibilities ... there are times when it is rational to desist from further reasoning; and gut feelings can help to set limits to our reflection, by excluding some options (those that are marked by a negative feeling) from further consideration.

Despite their mutual imbrication, the generation of gut feelings and their narrativization should not be conflated.

Religious practitioners orchestrate precise arrangements of somatic markers, "intersubjective structures of affect and memory," to diverse ends (Ó Tuathail 2003: 858). Ethnographies of Black Atlantic traditions document the existence of gut feelings and credit them with transmitting alarm or, conversely, with imparting reassurance at a visceral level (Le Reste et al. 2013). These hunches have a cognitive component, but they bypass rational deliberation to materialize in the abdomen as a low hum or bright tingle. Ethnographers tend to talk about having them more than they document them among interlocutors, but gut feelings do flit and spark through the archive (Houk 1995: 15; Lesshaff 2016: 67).

For example, they pop up in the story of a Middle Eastern immigrant to the United States recounting his growing attraction to Vodou: "'On the third week [at church], when I got up to leave, I saw this woman.' Clutching his belly, he says, 'I got this butterfly feeling in my stomach.' It turned out the woman attended St. Patrick's Cathedral and was also a Haitian Vodou priestess" (Harvey 2013).

Gut feelings are embedded in the account of more than one scholar-practitioner, heralding the advent of knowledge not arrived at through reason. Confronted with an ancestral Dominican "altar-punto," "a site of woven density," Ana-Maurine Lara (2020: 109–10) bears witness to its affective power:

> A vibe: that intangible ripple of energy, of something that you can feel in your gut, an awakening of intuition and knowing that is beyond the rational sphere. You *feel* it. In front of Lula's altar-punto, I am feeling a vibe. That vibe pulls me into the room and simultaneously out of time-space. That vibe tells me: those machetes mean something; they are doing something.[12]

For Lara, the altar's gut-level vibe testifies to its efficacy as a concentrated point of contact with sacred forces (a Vudú-Vodou *pwen*). In this case and others, a feeling in the gut not only indicates the possibility of "otherwise" cognition but embodies it. The gut feeling becomes ontologically consequential information. Practitioners talk about such feeling as a "proof" or confirmation – what Martin Holbraad (2008: 104) calls an "infinition" – that powers beyond the self exist within the self.

Gut feelings – and the aforementioned synonyms for and translations of this phrase – are nonetheless not as pervasive in the scholarship on Black Atlantic traditions as one might imagine. Their conspicuous absence seems at odds with the augmented role I am claiming for the gut. The inexact rendering of "gut feelings" into other languages may factor into this absence. Another viable reason for their scarcity is the limited vocabulary for discriminating between different types of sensations in the ethnographic and historical archive. Koen Stroeken (2008: 468) explains,

> As a Western ethnographer, I am inevitably influenced by Euro-American conceptions in which Aristotle's model of the five senses prevails (vision, hearing, smell, taste, touch). The model is based on bodily organs with *extero*ceptive orientation [and] overlooks *intero*ceptive sensations such as those pertaining to the stomach, oesophagus and intestines. Westerners tend to downplay interoceptive perception because of the seemingly limited information it provides about the external environment.

---

[12] Italics in the original.

Interoceptive perception has not been privileged as a site of corporeal discern-
ment in Afro-Atlantic sensorial regimes. As a consequence, when practitioners of Afro-Diasporic traditions do articulate some distinctions between
feelings in the gut and other forms of "visceral apprehension," they might not
be able to find the words to pinpoint the areas of greatest salience (Ochoa
2007: 492).

Yet I would hypothesize that the rarity of "gut feelings" in histories, oral
narratives, and ethnographies of Black Atlantic religions mainly derives from
the lack of a discourse on religious sincerity and sudden moments of conversion within them. These religions are characterized by practitioners' adoption
of the speech genre of "unchosen choice" as a condition of their socialization
(Pérez 2013a). Elders customarily relate their initiations not as something they
wanted to do, but something they had to do so as to save themselves or family
members from debilitating illness and imminent death: "I used to feel very bad ...
I had something in the stomach that didn't let me swallow. After I got
initiated [Lucumí], I felt much better and I didn't have any problemo"
(Viladrich 2009: 76). While this speech genre reflects the inhabitation of a
spirit idiom found in religions throughout the world, it may be historicized as
a collective response to the vilification of Afro-Diasporic traditions in the
late nineteenth and early twentieth centuries. As Lucumí, Palo Monte,
Candomblé, Vodou, and other African-inspired religions became synonymous
with barbarism and irrationality, it was preferable to cast initiation into them as
something one must do as a last resort – for one's health – than to admit a desire to
affiliate with them.

These traditions became stigmatized precisely through their association with
"bestial instinct" and subterranean urges (Cartwright 2013: 67, 185; Condé
1983: 7; Roumain [1944] 2000: 86). We have many early modern and
Enlightenment-era European commentators to blame for the stereotype of
Africa as a continent ruled entirely by base impulse and therefore without a
past. Relying on Willem Bosman's *A New and Accurate Description of the
Coast of Guinea, Divided into the Gold, Slave and Ivory Coasts* (1703),
Immanuel Kant concluded, "The negroes of Africa have, by their nature, no
feeling that rises above the trifling [also translated as coarse, foolish, very
profane, or banal]" (quoted in Smidt 2004: 110). An allegedly authoritative
assessment of Africans at close range, *A New and Accurate Description* identified "the fetish" as the key object of African worship, and perhaps G. W. F.
Hegel bears the greatest responsibility for amplification of Bosman's identification into a generalized theory of Black (un)civilization. In his posthumously
published *Lectures on the Philosophy of History* (1837), Hegel faults fetishism
(constructed as the opposite of religion) for Africa's "primitive" political

arrangements, cannibalistic habits, and mental enslavement. He abandons Africa as a land without Reason or history since its peoples' "sensuous arbitrariness" and arbitrary natures inhibit the development of long-term memory (Hegel [1837] 2001: 176–7).

These stereotypes of Africa would eventually extend to Afro-Diasporic religions so that animal sacrifice – to select but one example – would be inveighed against as the expression of bloodlust and spontaneous frenzy rather than the fastidiously prearranged, arduous execution of a regular religious obligation. Against this background of racist contempt for gut-level emotion among people of African descent, it is understandable that religious practitioners would not appeal to gut feeling in explanations of their religious decision-making. While outsiders to these traditions have commonly mentioned their own abdominal sensations as racialized responses to Black magic, ritual, and rhythm, few narratives exist in which practitioners themselves cite gut feelings (or analogous sensory impressions) as "somatic markers" that have helped them reach conclusions or arrive at moral-ethical judgments.

This does not mean that feelings in the gut and solar plexus do not have acute significance in Black Atlantic traditions. On the contrary, these sensations become media for communication between these entities and human beings after practitioners become versed in the intersubjective frames of reference supplied by the traditions in which they participate. Todd Ramón Ochoa (2007: 482) has written most lyrically of the sensations that betoken the dead's presence in the Kongo-inspired Afro-Cuban tradition Palo Monte:

> These were moments when Kalunga, the vast sea of the dead, the dead one, actualized in fluttering turns of the stomach, in goose bumps behind my arms, and in barely perceptible sensations in my chest, my throat, and in the muscles around my eyes. Over time I was instructed to acknowledge these everyday events in terms provided by Kalunga, the dead one.

"I can feel Kalunga right here, in my gut," Ochoa's (2010: 30) main interlocutor says. Elsewhere Ochoa (2010: 37) writes of the "ambient dead" as "a tension inside one's gut that runs up the nape of the neck," deftly sketching out the connection between feeling, affect, and emotion as they are experienced within Palo Monte.

In the interpretive apparatus furnished by Caribbean Espiritismo, nausea is among "one of the first signs of spirit presence" and the haptics of *fluidos* involve a "feeling of electrical charge, accelerated heart rate, pain and other symptoms felt at the corresponding body site, cool air blowing across the skin starting from the head, tingling, energy entering the stomach and leaving the head or moving like a snake in the body" (Thomas Csordas, cited in Espírito

Santo 2002: 143; Beliso-De Jesús 2015).[13] Practitioners of the Latin American María Lionza tradition also elaborate on *fluidos* and the gut in discourses of spirit possession. One Venezuelan medium, Daniel, is quoted as saying,

> The spirits, unless they are heavenly and cannot touch the earth because they are so elevated, they always enter your body through the feet, that is, from the bottom up, they go upwards ... and in the stomach ... here is where you feel the greatest influence, the greatest impact of the forces ... This is the basic point of elevation ... And according to be your spiritual and corporal purity, you will feel that the *fluidos* come good or bad ... Or, in that shock that is produced in the stomach, the force will not move on from there ... But if it doesn't move on from here, if it gets stuck in your stomach and doesn't go ... That is why one sees so many mediums forcing themselves, saying, *"Oh I can't [get fully possessed], and why..?"* Because the spirit, due to the impurities of the medium or for whatever reason, can't move on from there [the stomach]. (Martín and Rodero 2005: 270)[14]

The stomach detects the presence of a spirit but its complete incorporation depends on the spirit's ascension to the head, and that trajectory cannot be completed unless the medium's moral-ethical state and ritual proficiency will allow it. One subject of a study on Dominican Vudú-Vodou possession recalled mounting similarly, as "a specific feeling of energy" starting at the feet and "causing sensations in the stomach area before it would go up to the head" (quoted in Schaffler and Brabec de Mori 2017: 138–66). Some Vodouisants say that a deity that possesses devotees is "a lwa you receive in your stomach" (Brown 1995: 229).

In dominant secular discourses on gut feelings, they are characterized as raw, unaffected, and extemporaneous – the quintessence of genuine emotion. By contrast, in the "deep folklore" of Afro-Diasporic religions, feelings in the gut are narrated as having become intelligible as the result of a pedagogical process. Training by religious mentors is paramount in cultivating an awareness of such almost ineffable sensations, like "a feeling of un-attributable apprehension": "[M]y teachers taught me to affirm each definition, or aspect, of the dead, while affirming the others at once. In one moment the dead were discrete responsive entities such as a deceased parent or sibling ... Simultaneously, the dead were/ was a chill running up one's spine" (Ochoa 2005: 252). As Diana Espírito Santo (2015: 586) explains, "The education of the mediumship faculty involves, among other things, learning to discern the subtleties of [the] *fluido* and to be able to productively draw from it strings of valid information, insight, and imagery." Over time, muscle memories and recollections of gut feelings "may

---

[13] The quotation is identified as Raquel Romberg's in the text.
[14] Most of the ellipses here are reproduced from the original quotation.

become more and more 'enculturated,' leading to [deity]-specific 'somatic signatures'" in the context of spirit possession (Halloy 2012). Since practitioners learn that gut feelings express intimate relationships between themselves and their spirits, these sensations come to index the process of knowledge acquisition itself.

## 3 Gut Beings

In Afro-Diasporic religions, the gut is governed by specific deities and subject to ritual and ethnomedical intervention. Sensations in the gut do not stand for something outside the stomach, but instead call attention to a god, spirit, or ancestor materializing within it. Initially frustrated by his main interlocutor's refusal to assign symbolic meaning to gut feelings, Ochoa (2010: 31) says,

> At her insistence, it took an epistemological leap to realize that grasping the value Isidra placed on the dead would require taking her *literally* when she said the dead were in her gut. Isidra considered everyday experiences such as sleeplessness and pangs of anxiety not as "signs" of the dead but as versions of the dead in themselves.

Black Atlantic traditions observe what I have, in the context of Lucumí, called an ethnosymptomatology: "an understanding of the body based on the ownership of its constituent parts by different orishas, and predicated on the idea that the orishas may use their 'property' for the purposes of signification" (Pérez 2016; also see Maffi 1994). Although this formulation was developed with reference to one Afro-Cuban religious formation, it applies more broadly to Black Atlantic traditions characterized by spirit possession, initiation, and the speech genre of "unchosen choice." Practitioners construct symptoms of affliction as both signs of favor and exasperated bids for attention from ancestors and deities. To trust one's gut, then, is to know the being(s) within it.

Black Atlantic deities preside over discrete parts of the body. The stomach as a digestive organ has a well-documented association with Afro-Diasporic gods related to Legba (like Exú and Elegguá); in West African Ewe-Fon traditions, "the messenger and trickster god Legba 'stays in the navel where he amuses himself by causing anger'" (Le Herissé, quoted in Blier 1996: 145). In Brazilian Candomblé, the female *orixás* Iemanjá and Oxum "own" the lower and upper abdomen, respectively. In Lucumí, Yemayá and Ochún do. These deities mark their territory by creating uncomfortable and disruptive symptoms. Sufferers seek out ritual specialists to get rid of their pain but, more often than not, they wind up assigning meaning to it (whether it stays or goes). Joseph Murphy (1993: 66–7) was told by an Ifá diviner,

An upset stomach is connected to a confused head … "You must become skeptical. Observant. You must listen to your head." An upset stomach means that Oshun, the *orisha* of abdominal organs, is speaking to me. "She is behind you. Pray to her. Ask her for things. Thank her. She is calling you."[15]

Some aspects of this depiction are transatlantically characteristic of Ochún – one Yorùbá praise song for Ọṣun says, "She smites the belly of the liar with her bell" – but her relationship to human infirmity mirrors that of other Afro-Diasporic deities and ancestors (Pierre Verger, quoted in Thompson 1983: 80). The progression sketched out by Murphy may be schematized as follows: identification of a symptom with a god, spirit, or ancestor; interpretation of the symptom as mandating a change in conduct; and affirmation that the god, spirit, or ancestor is "speaking" – or even shouting – through the affliction they have inflicted.

In the Afro-Cuban tradition of Arará, the *foldun* (*vodun*) Neggé is said to rule the stomach (Brown 1989: 504; Moliner 2013: 75).[16] In Haitian Vodou, the *lwas* Ogou, Danbala, Ezili Freda, and the Marasa (divine twins) interface with the stomach in different ways. For example, Ezili and the Marasa are associated with *migan*, "a ritualistic potion prepared with the blood of sacrificed animals, sugar, and spices" meant to be ingested for protection from harm (Hebblethwaite 2012). It is confected by someone possessed by Ezili: "Erzulie holds and kills the pig whose blood will be used with other ingredients to make a drink (*migan*) with a magical character" (Begot 1980: 105). It heals the stomach by forcing the one who ingests it to vomit up any poison or bad magic they may have unwittingly consumed.[17] This detail might help us decode the gesture made by those mounted by Ogou in possession, when they dance with a sabre or machete and push the point against their stomach until they bend the blade (Burton 1997: 251). These Ogous may be dramatizing their (and their servants') imperviousness to sorcery, as well as the masculine hardness and heartiness of their guts.

The literature on Afro-Jamaican "folk beliefs" and religious formations is replete with references to the gut. In Jamaican folk medicine, "Stomach ailments [are] the largest category of complaints" and have traditionally been ameliorated through herbal remedies, especially infused baths and "bush teas" (Payne-Jackson and Alleyne 2004: 98). According to Elisa J. Sobo (1993: 38–9),

The most important part of the inner body is the *belly*, where blood is made. This big cavity or bag extends from just below the breast to the pelvis. The belly is full of bags and tubes, such as the baby bag and the urine tube …

---

[15] At least one Diloggún diviner ties stomach upset to castigation: "You are sick in your belly or legs[;] it is a punishment from Òshùn" (Madan 2021[2005]: 209).

[16] Angarica (1955: 14) defines Neggé as a path of the *fodun/orisha* Babalú Ayé.

[17] Personal communication, Dr. Eziaku Nwokocha, July 29, 2021.

The "stomach," which is a cavity and not a food bag, is located just above the "belly" at the chest or breast – the area where the heart and "mind" are. The "mind" is the seat of volition, agency, and intention. A person often says s/he will go somewhere or do a thing "if my mind tell [*sic*] me." The brain or "marrow," located in the head, is simply a computational tool and a storage space for facts.

These ideas are woven into the ritual practices of Myal, Kumina, Revival Zion, and even Rastafari.

Converts to Christianity do not jettison these corporeal topographies but recast them within a gendered Protestant or Roman Catholic interpretive framework. Jamaican Pentecostal women say of the ritual "in-filling" of the Holy Spirit: "The Spirit come up through the belly and reach like blood to the heart" (Austin-Broos 1997: 133). Pentecostal women somaticize religious experience to a greater extent than men do: "Women underscore the experience of envelopment that starts with a presence in the belly, moves to 'touch' the heart, and pushes itself through the mouth as the transformation and incorporation are accomplished" (Austin-Broos 1997: 138). Christian practitioners of Guyanese Komfa relate body parts to specific ancestral spirits, saints, biblical prophets, and apostles for the purpose of dream interpretation and healing. While Faith, Imagination, Understanding, Will, and Zeal are located in different areas of the brain and head above the nose, the alimentary tract is shared by three apostles: "James (son of Zebedee)" governs "Wisdom – Pit of stomach", "James (son of Alphaeus)" controls "Order – Navel", and Thaddeus oversees "Elimination – Abdominal region" (Gibson 2001: 83). "Thus an abdominal illness will be healed by praying to Thaddeus," Kean Gibson (2001: 83) writes.

In the Surinamese Winti tradition, some spirits manifest in the gut. "The Papa-*winti* causes women to develop a *winti*-bere, a big belly, because the snake comes to live in the belly; an Apuku also causes a big belly filled with blood" (Wooding 1981: 128).[18] In the 1930s, Melville J. Herskovits and Frances K. Herskovits (1934: 267) documented the physical impact of different protective medicines (*obias*) depending on the spiritual entity empowered by them, such that "The Vodu [*obia* goes] into the belly." H. U. E. Thoden van Velzen and Wilhelmina van Wetering (2004: 25) maintain that "Until about 1970 the

---

[18] *Bere* means "belly" and denotes a matrilineal group (sometimes rendered as "extended family") in Suriname (Thoden van Velzen and van Wetering 2004: 28; Wekker 2006: 114). Among Central African Ndembu people, "stomach (ivumu)" "also means 'womb' and 'matrilineage,'" "comprising a woman and her descendants," precisely because "in Ndembu ideas of anatomy, the stomach and the womb are not clearly distinguished" (Turner 1978: 566; Chock 1967: 76). Abdominal and uterine illnesses are still associated by some Surinamese with the presence of a Vodu/Fodu spirit, carried through family lines, that resides in the stomach. See "Fodu of .... ???" *Winti Praktÿk [Praktijk] Baaswaterval*, June 30, 2011, https://winti.baaswaterval.nl/winti-fodu/14/fodu-of/7820.

Ndyuka recognized four main pantheons: the *Yooka* (ancestors), *Papagadu* or *Vodu* (reptile spirits), *Ampuku* (forest spirits) and *Kumanti* (warrior spirits)," adding, "Except for the Kumanti spirit, all may turn into *kunu* (avenging spirits) when offended or to redress human sins or negligence." The stomach houses these *kunu*, variously translated as "hereditary gods" or cultural "curses." Markus Balkenhol (2021: 265) quotes author and scholar Edgar Cairo on the stigma that once accompanied participation in Afro-Surinamese religions:

> Because far too little research was being done on one's own culture, that data was lost, afraid as one was to gain dishonor with "dumb-superstitious negro-like things." … Even worse: if one got involved with the negro thing you would never get rid of it! Evil spirits … they would hatefully target you! You would never stop to "dance Winti and serve Thingy in superstition!" You were cursed, cursed with the kunu [curse] of the negro's belly![19]

"Belly" here is a synecdoche for the very existence of Black Surinamese people, coerced by European colonial discourses into rejecting their religious pasts as humiliating and their ancestral spirits as malevolent.

The stomach's simultaneous susceptibility and sacrality are evoked by Catalan artist Antoni Miralda's reliquary sculpture *Sant Stomak* (2015), inspired by a Catholic *ex-voto* that he found in a museum's archives (Figure 1).[20] Latin American and Caribbean traditions such as Espiritismo and Mexican/Xicanx *curanderismo* have long assumed that the stomach is especially prone to volt sorcery and mystical aggression. Their practitioners have diagnosed a number of culturally specific conditions that respond to ethnobotanical preparations and the curative techniques of healers taught through intergenerational apprentice-ships. One ailment, *empacho*, is generally assumed to be an intestinal blockage; its "main symptom is a feeling of a 'balloon in the stomach' associated with abdominal pain" (Swartz 2010: 70). A *sobador(a)* is a healer who specializes in performing massages and applying acupressure, particularly on the belly, to alleviate *empacho* and other abdominal ailments or to promote fertility. Hand massages called *santigüos* may be prescribed for a range of illnesses traced to the alimentary tract. In therapeutic encounters, the gut speaks, making its complaints and rumblings of distress as audible as "gastric upsets ('griping in the guts') caused by bad food" (Thomas 1971: 7).[21]

---

[19] Cairo's words echo William Shakespeare's *The Merchant of Venice* (Act III, Scene V), which refers to the pregnancy of an African maidservant as "the getting up of the Negro's belly."

[20] In 1984, Miralda debuted *Santa Comida*, an installation inspired by the *orisha*s' food offerings. It was mounted at the Museo del Barrio in New York with the assistance of African-American scholar and priest Baba John Mason.

[21] Some local healers have used a child's placenta and the desiccated remnants of their umbilical cord to heal that child (Cabrera [1954] 1968: 260).

**Figure 1** *Sant Stomak* by Antoni Miralda, FoodCultura Satellite Boquería, reproduced with the kind permission of the artist.

While healers and herbalists are summoned to cure illness, sufferers often have recourse to diviners, especially when the underlying etiologies remain in doubt after unsuccessful allopathic treatments. Through in-depth diagnosis, diviners pinpoint not only what a client's problem is but also why they are experiencing that particular problem at that particular time. Diviners refer to the gut in both a biomedical register and symbolically rich spirit idioms that trace digestive complaints back to clients' patron deities. The two most comprehensively documented Black Atlantic divination systems are Ifá and Diloggún, both of Yorùbá origin and most often practiced in the context of Afro-Cuban and Black American styles of *orisha* worship.[22] In the absence of information on other divination systems, perhaps a handful of examples from the Diloggún or "sixteen cowries" system will serve to establish the alimentary tract as a prime divinatory concern.

---

[22] This discussion cannot be considered complete without including the *chamalongo* and *vititi mensu* oracles of the Afro-Cuban *reglas de congo*; the *barajas españolas* (Spanish cards) used in Espiritismo, Vodou, and Dominican Vudú/la Veintiuna División; and divination methods like the reading of tobacco leaves.

A number of Diloggún verses, or *odu*, caution against eating foods tabooed in previous divinations and flag issues with parasites, hernias, gas, inflammation, and constipation, in addition to menstrual cramps and uterine disorders. For example, receiving the divination sign Okana Merindilogún (1–16) "is a sign of abdominal and intestinal trouble, and when it opens … it is not unusual for the client to experience minor stomach discomfort before [the reading] closes" (Lele 2003: 85). Oche Eyioko (5–2) advises, "Be careful with your belly and your guts," and Oshe Meji (5–5) brings news of "bound [tied up or twisted] intestines and problems with digestion of foods, the acid in the stomach and ulcers" (Madan [2005] 2021: 212; Omi olo Oshun 2009, unpaginated). Several *odu* forbid the eating of foods made with animal intestines (like sausages) and more than a dozen *odu* warn of intestinal ailments.[23] In Nicolas Valentin Angarica's 1955 *Manual de Oriate Religión Lucumí*, about seventy *odu* – almost a third of the 256 possible combinations of signs – mention the stomach's fragility and gastric illnesses. The high number of references to the stomach in Angarica's text may be accounted for by the fact that it was meant to serve as a guide for initiatory divinations and it repeats details that other texts omit for the sake of brevity.[24] But every compilation of Diloggún verses I have examined puts the gut and its health (or lack thereof) in the gods' and ancestors' hands.

## 4 Gut History

Gut history! What is it? It is history from the inside out … history that talks from the inside out – with guts … We struggle for more than getting a pat on the head from "ethnic" historians or similar "objective" people. Their style of history presents only half of the story. But gut history makes the invisible visible. If this society is to be a harmonious one, then we must know where we came from.

*Xiaoping Li (2007: 36–7)*

Before engaging further with the gut in Afro-Diasporic religions, we must bow to some historical antecedents in the theory and praxis of Yorùbá, Ewe-Fon, and Kongo peoples. These are the African groups generally recognized as having contributed most heavily to the formation of initiatory Black Atlantic traditions through the knowledge transmitted by enslaved peoples and their descendants.

---

[23] For example, Ojuani (also spelled Owani) says, "Don't eat grains or intestines [*tripas*]" (Cámara 2009: 63; Castrillo 2006: 136). Intestines appear more than a dozen times in both Lele 2003 and Angarica 1955.

[24] Another factor might be Angarica's fidelity to fleshing out the implications of the double cast of Diloggún rendered in a compound form referred to as "tonti." See *Centro de Estudios Lukumí*, April 21, 2021, https://bit.ly/3gnMreA, and u/gears_wrecks-48, "Can someone explain the thought process that Diloggun diviners in Santeria are not reading traditional Diloggun but are actually reading Odu Ifa through Diloggun?" June 8, 2021. https://bit.ly/3TJNy6O.

A more thorough discussion would add Igbo, Kromanti, and Cross-River peoples to the list of those whose precedents shaped Black Atlantic configurations of embodiment. But even if there were no space constraints to prevent us from considering the full range of influential ethnic groups, this is no easy conversation.

The possibility of unearthing the roots of Afro-Diasporic practices has been the subject of debate for more than a century. Melville J. Herskovits's 1940s argument concerning the presence of "survivals" in Afro-American religions has continued to hold great sway, despite its essentialization of cultural forms (Mintz and Price [1976] 1992). Many scholars have nevertheless wrestled with defining the relationship between morphologically similar African and Afro-Diasporic cultural expressions. For example, Stephan Palmié (2013) has questioned whether Lucumí can be called Afro-Cuban given the tradition's globalization and the diversity of its practitioners even within Cuba itself.

I proceed with the conviction that tribute must be paid and credit given to African peoples and their Black descendants for the emergence of Afro-Diasporic religions. Attributions of origins are always political, and seldom more so than when speaking of Yorùbá ethnogenesis – and the fact that *Yorùbá* was not widely used for a coherent cultural aggregate until the early twentieth century. There is also the problem of juggling nineteenth-, twentieth-, and twenty-first-century historical and ethnographic sources about geographically distinct places and peoples. Such comparative moves have sometimes been undertaken as if no change had taken place on the African continent since the precolonial period, and without accounting for societal crises and historical developments as the direct result of the transatlantic slave trade and colonialism as well as internal factors unrelated to European predation, exploitation, and "necropolitics" (Mbembe 2003). It is folly to draw a direct line from a royal shrine room in the old Oyo Empire to the *igbodu* (sacred grove) of an initiation on the South Side of Chicago. But it is more foolish to assert that there is no line at all.

The line does not have to be linear, as if there is a stable "before" (Herskovits's "baseline") and "after" (i.e., now) that straightforwardly prove the existence of a temporally antecedent pattern (Apter 1991). Documented histories of transatlantic travel and transcultural collaboration put to rest the idea that Afro-Diasporic religions contain only the intellectual and material resources that enslaved Africans had at their disposal (Matory 2005). In pointing out the similarity between Yorùbá, Ewe-Fon, and Kongo attitudes toward the gut and those to be found in Afro-Diasporic religions, I am indicating a range of complex reticulations that may be traced to different historical moments. It is possible that some superficial resemblances derive from simple coincidences. It is probably the case that centuries-old religious exchanges in West Africa led to the worship of related deities within analogous religious systems.

Practitioners have theorized on these matters no less than scholars have (Palmié 2013). Eugenio Matibag (1996: 26) points out,

> [Lydia] Cabrera quotes one of her informants, called "the mother of [Lucumí elder Teresa Muñoz] Omí Tomi," as saying, "Lucumi, Arara, Dahomey and Mina, all are akin. All understood one another although their languages were different. But their Saints are similar. They would go from one land to another."

Although philologist Max Müller has often been called "the father of comparative religion," ordinary people in the intensely multireligious spaces of the African Diaspora have been shrewd comparativists, discerning patterns across cultures through feature-by-feature analysis while factoring in variables like the incommensurability of local categories, divergent historical imaginations, and points of stark contrast. Cabrera identified the mother of Omí Tomí, one of Cabrera's steadfast interlocutors, as a formerly enslaved "Mina Popó [Fon]" woman "from the Slave Coast to the west of Dahomey" (Matibag 1996: 27). She would have been aware that the Oyo Empire and the kingdoms of Dahomey not only spread their religious formations through "soft power" like cultural diplomacy, ceremonial pageantry, gift exchange, and economic trade but also imposed them through imperial aggression (Brown 2003: 215). The arrangement of Afro-Diasporic pantheons and ritual speech (such as praise songs) register the frictions and affinities between rival ethnic groups in the precolonial period.

Across a number of West and Central African cultures, shared sensibilities extended to religiously laden conceptions of the body and its senses. Among these are attitudes toward the gut. I am far from the first to make this connection, for which some have found evidence in the records of ecclesiastical chroniclers:

> Diego Torres de Vargas, in his ... *Description of Puerto Rico* (1647), says: "In the time of governor Gabriel de Roxas [1608], it came to pass that a Black woman had a spirit that spoke to her in her stomach. She was taken to the church and exorcized, and the spirit gave his name as Pedro Lorenzo. And when questioned he spoke of obscure and occult things ... and the commissioner of the Inquisition ordered him not to speak on pain of excommunication. And then another [spirit] was discovered, and if the first was to be marveled at, the second one and the others that later came out were paid scant attention.
>
> "Black women say that they have them, that in their land [*tierra*] the spirits enter their womb in the visible form of a small animal and that they are

inherited one generation to the other, becoming their patron spirits [*mayorazgo*]." (Méndez [1964] 1970): 60)[25]

Raquel Romberg (2007: 82) glosses this passage as follows:

> We can now recognize these colonial reports about spirit possession in recent work on Cameroonian witch craft [*sic*], according to which the spirit is believed to appear in an animal form, located in the belly and genetically inherited through female lines ([Peter] Geschiere 1997), evidence that also resonates with work on Afro-Latin religions in the Americas.

It may be that the Black women in Torres de Vargas's account were in fact from present-day Cameroon. But a large number of precolonial African cultures appear to have given the stomach a larger role in spirit possession – and the ownership of spirits – than the current overriding emphasis on the head would lead one to believe.

Yorùbá and Ewe-Fon traditions contributed heavily to Afro-Diasporic traditions of *orisha/orixá*, *lwa*, and *fodun* worship. Miguel W. Ramos (2011: 45) appeals to Yorùbá concepts to delineate the gut's sacrality in Lucumí:

> It is said that Ipín Ijeún [the stomach] is the most demanding "orisha" that exists since it requests daily sacrifices. It usually warns its owner of events before they happen. The so-called "tickle in the stomach" that many people feel when an imminent danger is approaching or they experience a fright or feel romantically or sexually attracted to another person are manifestations or direct messages of this energy. Also, ijeún and inú are associated with inventiveness, strength, and bravery ... The one who lacks initiative is *Kò n'ifun ninu* – he has no intestines – or, in good Cuban, "no tiene gandinga," very similar to the English *lack of guts* – lack of intestines.[26]

Ramos also defines the Yorùbá-derived term *ipori* as the "spirit of the relationship between the physical and the spiritual ([that] lives in the stomach)" (Madan [2005] 2021: 105; Medina and Hernández 1995: 25).

In the late 1950s, Lydia Cabrera ([1957] 1986: 220–1) listed Lucumí definitions for *inú* that implicate the alimentary tract from the oral cavity to the intestines:

> *Inó, inú, ilú*: The entrails, viscera.
> *Ino obiri*: Matrix.
> *Inú*: Tongue.
> *Inú*: Speech.
> *Inú*: Heart, chest.
> *Inú, imo*: Mouth.
> *Inú*: Inside.

---

[25] I have found the name rendered as both Diego Torres de Vargas and Diego de Torres Vargas.
[26] Relatedly, in Spanish, to be *de malas entrañas* – "of bad entrails" – means to be malicious or hateful.

Cabrera appears to have relied heavily on missionary and linguist Samuel Ajayi Crowther's (1843: 132) *Vocabulary of the Yoruba Language*, which defines *Inọ̀, Inu* as "matrice, matrix, breast-venter, disposition; the inside, mind, thought, womb, belly, entrails, hollowness, stomach." Similarly, Cabrera ([1957] 1986: 209) defines *Ikún* as "intestines" and "garbage" (undoubtedly due to the customary disposal of the intestines after animals are butchered), adding that *Ikún Baba Orisha* is "food for the filling up of the orishas." Crowther (1843: 125) defines *Ikùn* as "belly, stomach, abdomen, the main ventricle" and appends the saying *Ikùn babba òrìṣa* with the translation, "The belly is the chief of the gods, because it claims the first attention."

It is impossible to determine to what extent the terms published by Cabrera were in use among Afro-Cuban religious practitioners in the mid-twentieth century, and with what degree of fidelity Crowther – a Bible translator – rendered the words of his Yorùbá compatriots. But Crowther's proverb finds corroboration in the work of British Army officer and ethnographer Alfred B. Ellis (1894: 126–7), who half a century later identified *ipin ijeun* as the deification of the stomach (connected with "fire-worship"), through which hunger (*ebi*) is communicated.[27] Contemporary commentator Ajayi Kehinde Temitope Emmanuel (2017: 13) contends that "Ellis misinterpreted a common Yoruba proverb which is usually taken as a joke – *Orisa bi ofun ko si, ojojumo ni gb'ebo*," asserting that "The point of the statements simply emphasizes the physical need of man that he has to eat regularly and literally every day to live or survive." While bearing in mind these misgivings about the "ipin ijeun," other Yorùbá sources do corroborate a linkage between the belly, fiery emotion, pleasure, character, and spiritual power (Soyinka 2002).

Suzanne Preston Blier (2015: 170) quotes William Bascom on the stomach's historical prominence in Yorùbá sculpture:

> A person who would be called cool-headed in English, one who is even tempered and "keeps his cool," is spoken of as "one who has a soft belly" (*oninu riro*); whereas a hot-headed person, who is quick tempered and easily offended is called "one who has a hard belly" (*oninu lile*). The stomach can cause a man to lose his temper and become involved in a fight which will spoil his luck or "spoil his head."

Speaking of the contemporary moment, anthropologist Emmanuel D. Babatunde (1992: 92–3) writes,

> Kindness, *inú-rere*, literally means either "a good stomach and heart" – what constitutes for the Yoruba the totality of the physical things within man – or "a

---

[27] Ellis was a colonial military administrator who embraced white supremacist notions of racial difference and believed that, when Europeans arrived in Africa, they gave "natives" the idea of God (Ellis 1887: 6; Healy 1998: 108–9).

good inside (stomach)" ... Inú, the stomach, is also the repository for witchcraft paraphernalia.[28]

Linguist Mark Dingemanse (2006: 44–5) takes an etymological approach to analysis of the gut:

> Inú "belly, inside" figures in a host of expressions relating to emotional and cognitive states and qualities of persons ... The generality of inú as compared to ikun "stomach," the wide variety of functions ascribed to it, as well as the overlap of some of these with other internal organs might be explained partly by understanding inú more like a containing region ("the inside") than a discrete internal body-part. This also accords with Afoláyan's description of inú as "a huge storage space that houses wisdom and words of knowledge."

Dingemanse (2006: 45) further notes that *ikùn* relates to "digestion of food" while *inú* as "belly, inside" is used in expressions about "good feelings (sweet); bad feelings (blocked); anger (stirred up); thinking" and a lack of *ìfun*, "intestine," is cited to denote cowardice. It may be a stretch to connect this continental African ethnographic material to Afro-Diasporic religious formations of a century prior and an ocean away. Yet this is not the only set of sources that accord with conceptualizations of the gut-brain axis in Afro-Diasporic religions.

Turning to the sources on Ewe-Fon traditions, Suzanne Preston Blier (1996: 163) has written at tremendous length about the degree to which Ewe-Fon peoples have historically emphasized the stomach: "More than any other body feature, the stomach (*ho, homε, xo, xomε*) is perceived as anatomical and aesthetic bearer of the emotions." Blier marshals an impressive amount of linguistic and ritual evidence to argue that the stomach should not be viewed in isolation from other organs but as an anatomical aggregate. Blier (1996: 142) quotes Claude Rivière: "Language reveals that the stomach, as identified with the intestines (*dɔmε*), is the psychological seat of the sentiments."[29]

As "a principal locus of the emotions," the stomach holds the heat of anger as well as other sentiments that, according to social convention, should be concealed (Blier 1996: 293). Because the interior of the stomach is not visible, it is the quintessential hiding place for simmering rancor and scorching rage, as well as other feelings whose revelation would cause social conflict. For this reason, the guts are "referred to frequently in the context of divination" and Ewe-Fon oracular paraphernalia alludes to the relationship between the stomach and speech: "Significantly, *atε* is the term for both the board used in Fa divination

---

[28] The belly is the traditional location of witchcraft substance(s) in several African cultures, especially among cisgender women.

[29] Blier (1996: 139) also cites Roberto Pazzi to this effect.

consultation ... and the platters on which market women display food" (Blier 1996: 144). One diviner, named Ayido, told Blier (1996: 144): "If Fa glances over ... all the words that are in the stomach of the [client], Fa sees them all and begins to say them. As the *atɛ* also looks into the stomach of Fa, *atɛ* will say all that is in the stomach."

The bulk of these data appears to associate the gut with emotion to the seeming exclusion of cognition, but, in most cases, Blier's examples involve knowledge of one's feelings, verbal articulation of this knowing, and what one might call the psychological "processing" of experiences of which one is cognizant. The kidneys, conceived of as part of the gut, do most of the intellectual labor: "The *ayi* 'gives thought to the head. That is why the word *ayi* frequently has the sense of intelligence'" (Guérin Montilus, quoted in Blier 1996: 146). Blier (1996: 145–6) explains,

> Emotional and aesthetic values identified with the stomach, whether generally or with the navel in particular find important complements in the lower abdomen and specifically the kidneys (*ayi, ai*), which are identified as a primary organ of reflection. According to Guédou ... "The term *ayi* signifies the spirit, conscience, advice, attention, conduct, character, and moral disposition in general ... the [*ayi*] is thus the seat of life, reason, and conscience."

Fon phrases that refer to *ayi* include "seek to understand," "examine your conscience," and "think of something" (Blier 1996: 146). Blier (1996: 391n26) adds, "The word *ayi* in many Fon texts is translated as 'heart' because in the West it is this organ which is most closely identified with the conscience and the sentiments."

*Ayi* is not only the "source of all sentiment and thought," it is the "seat of one's personal vodun," as Blier (1995: 67) asserts in a discussion of Fon precedents in Haitian Vodou. This may be one of the reasons – somewhat understated in Blier's account of the ritual sculptures called *bociɔ* – for the abdomen's protrusion in magico-religious figures that are activated by special substances for protective and curative purposes. *Bociɔ* share a family resemblance to Kongo *minkisi* (singular: *nkisi*), "power objects" historically commissioned from healers, or *nganga*, among inhabitants of the Kingdom of Kongo and throughout Bantu-speaking coastal Central African groups. The stomach's physical saliency in *minkisi* matches its medical and cosmological prominence. Like *bociɔ*, *minkisi* have been made to perform such tasks as enforcing law contracts and ensuring the maintenance of domestic harmony. They have most often taken the shape of human beings with a distinctive proportional ratio that accentuates the midsection, which is hollowed out and filled with ritually charged substances such as herbs, soil, beads, chalk or white clay, and feathers.

Wyatt MacGaffey (MacGaffey et al. 1993: 65) says of *minkisi*,

> The belly (*mooyo*, which also means life or soul) is an obviously appropriate place for medicines. They are usually sealed in with resin; the medicine pack often has a mirror on the outside as a divination device.

The behavior of *minkisi* in response to affliction is identical to that of Afro-Diasporic deities like Ochún:

> Each person chooses an *nkisi* to correspond to his illness. One would not, for example, take *nkisi* Mwe Nsundi for a headache. For a pain in the stomach one would not take *nkisi* Mbwanga. Whichever nkisi causes the trouble, that is the one which gives the cure.
>
> (Nsemi, Cahier 391, quoted in MacGaffey et al. 1993: 63)

This sensibility is reflected in the relationship of Afro-Cuban *paleros* – initiates within Palo Monte, Palo Mayombe, Kimbisa, and other *reglas de congo* – toward their *nganga*s. A *nganga* is an iron cauldron that holds the spirit of a deceased person (*nfumbi*) in its belly. A *nganga* is also identified with a Kongo deity (*mpungu*) who embodies ancestral, geographical, and cosmological forces.

Kongo traditions formed the basis for the *reglas de congo* in Cuba and Candomblé Angola in Brazil, and impacted a host of other traditions like Haitian Vodou and even the Black Spiritual Church (Rey and Richman 2010; Wehmeyer 2000). Inspired by MacGaffey's work, Eugenio Matibag (1996: 172) ties "Kongo biometaphysical anatomy" to the contemporary ethos of the *reglas de congo*:

> For the Bakongo, the soul inside, called *nsala*, animates the body; it is also identified with breath and shadow, but the *nsala* is centered in the heart ... and has the ability to leave and establish itself elsewhere. The belief in the *nsala*'s mobility supports the belief that souls of the departed may be summoned through the work of a *nganga*-cauldron. Also residing within the body is the *mooyo*, focused in the stomach or belly, charged with feeding the rest of the body.

This overview maps the *nganga*'s functioning isomorphically onto the human body, giving the gut pride of place. Paleros are famous for their extensive knowledge of herbal remedies to soothe the stomach; less well known is the ritual ingestion of the *sopa nganga* ("soup of the *nganga*," also called "soup of the dead" or "soup of the godmother"), the ingredients of which index those of the *nganga* assembled for an initiate (Alpizar and Calleja 2019: 106). Like the Haitian *migan*, the *sopa nganga* is meant to protect the stomach (referred to as *entún* or *bumo*) from penetration by witchcraft by causing vomiting, thereby ejecting any bad magic. Although "many Bantu languages employ the root *\*-bumo* to connote 'belly,'" it has sometimes been translated as "heart," like *ayi* in the Fon context (Giles-Vernick 1999: 320n32).

These associations still leave us at some distance from a gut history that could deliver a definitive idea of where the gut(s) in Afro-Diasporic religions "came from." If we can suspend our disbelief for a moment – and relax the hermeneutics of our suspicion – the aforementioned historical precedents and historically proximate concurrences above do seem to hint at some speculative linkages. But we must bear in mind that any attempt to connect Black Atlantic traditions and continental African corporeal knowledges is in itself evidence of attachment to a discourse of cultural authenticity. In forging a logical chain from the conceptual concatenations suggested by comparative studies, this section may only disclose the desire of various scholars (including the present author) to marvel at "an obscure miracle of connection" (Kamau Brathwaite, quoted in Scott 1999; Apter 2018). The alluring similarities may be an optical illusion, a false enlightenment that pledges in vain to dispel the darkness of origins that are not only opaque but irrecuperable.

## 5 Gut Delicacy

> Each particular Person hath his peculiar False God, which he or she worships after their manner, on that Day of the Week on which he was born ... Most of the *Negroes*, especially the Principal, have besides this another weekly day sanctified to their *Fetiche*'s. On these Days they kill a Cock, and sometimes, if they are rich, a Sheep, which they offer up to their God in words alone; for they immediately fall upon it and tear it to pieces with their Fingers ...
>
> The Guts they cut into small pieces, and squeezing out the Excrement with their Fingers, they boil it together with the Lungs, Liver, and Heart, with a little Salt and Malaget, or Guinea Pepper, without washing it from the Blood. This they call Eyntjeba, and it is esteemed the greatest Delicacy that can be dressed up.
>
> *Willem Bosman (1705: 153–4)*

Few books about Africa have been as influential – and as detrimental to people of African descent – as the aforementioned *A New and Accurate Description of the Coast of Guinea*, written by Dutch Calvinist merchant and seafarer Willem Bosman. The frontispiece for the English edition folds out into a copperplate engraving of West Africa by cartographer Herman Moll, and the volume was intended to map its inhabitants' relationship to material objects and each other along Protestant Christian coordinates. Among other dubious achievements, Bosman's oft-reprinted text succeeded in popularizing the "fetish" as the focal point of African worship (Pietz 1988). Bosman charged Africans with the inability to fathom and properly reckon economic value, even as the transatlantic slave trade – reliant on the legal status of captive Africans as property – approached its zenith. He also chalked up the phenomenon of spirit possession to the deceptions of African women (Johnson 2011).

Several noteworthy studies have followed Bosman's extensive trail through Enlightenment philosophy and social theory (Matory 2018). The passage just reproduced appears to be a continuation of the attacks on animal sacrifice in previous pages and precedes his famously disparaging remarks on the similarities between African "Feticheers" and European Roman Catholics, given their food taboos (among other purported parallels between them). Bosman's striking tableau was meant to inspire intense disgust and visceral revulsion, dramatizing the extent to which the foul habits of Africans differ from those of civilized non-"Negroes." The indelicate picture he paints of dung (*drek* in the original Dutch) manually removed from gory animal intestines (*darmen*) and cooked "without washing" was intended to make readers recoil. He wanted them to clutch their stomachs, stick out their tongues, puff out their cheeks, gag, throw up in their mouths a little bit, and otherwise physically react to the horrors that he relates.[30]

Which local term Bosman transcribed as "Eyntjeba" is anyone's guess, assuming there was a signified to his sign and that he did not pull this word out of thin air. The organs that Bosman names – lungs, liver, and heart – are, however, still among those offered to Afro-Diasporic deities today. They may not be seasoned in the manner Bosman specified, and they are certainly washed, yet they are esteemed a great delicacy, at least for the deities whose palates must be sated. Despite the ethnographic ubiquity of Black Atlantic sacrificial cuisines, dishes that contain the abdominal membranes and intestines have yet to be theorized in terms of their liturgical or ideological importance. What they might say about practitioners' guts in relation to the gods, spirits, and ancestors has not been a matter of speculation. For this reason, I now pivot to a delicate consideration of Afro-Diasporic ritual practices, with particular attention to the "sister religions" of Lucumí and Candomblé and their spiritual cousin Vodou.

Not all Black Atlantic traditions (such as Rastafari) rely on "life offerings," but sacrifice is essential in initiatory formations that consecrate objects to embody the deities, ordain practitioners into a priesthood, and expect them to "mount" devotees in spirit possession (Thornton 2021). The way to the spirits' hearts is through their stomachs, as evinced by the proliferation of religious cuisines, cooking techniques, and protocols for ritual alimentation observed throughout the African Diaspora. By catering to them, practitioners "fill the

---

[30] *Drek en darmen*, "dung and intestines," was rendered "Garbage and Excrements" in the first English translation (1705: 151).

hungry bellies, slake the dry throats, and stroke the wounded pride of the ancestors and the [deities]" (Brown 2001: 52). But these entities are discriminating connoisseurs and care must be taken to feed them in keeping with their preferences. Their hunger is taken as literally existing – a social fact to be discounted at one's peril – and its satisfaction depends on catering to their idiosyncrasies. In Palo Monte,

> Independently from the complex process of assemblage, pots are regularly fed and in cases when food is too hard, it is softened with some softer components, such as the blood of a dove or honey, so that mystic digestion does not become difficult and the *nganga* [sacred cauldron] turns whimsical and unforeseeable for some time. (Miletti-González 2013: 665)

The spirits' nourishment determines their future behavior. They respond to the degree that practitioners anticipate their desires and invest generously in the proper functioning of their alimentary tracts (Stevens 1995).

No less important are the micropractices of butchering, cleaning, and cooking that transform bare flesh into sacred fare. The deities themselves endorse and empower this process. Most often, the spirit connected to sacrificial cuisine is blacksmith and master of the forge Ogún/Ogum/Ogou. John Mason (1997: 362) identifies Ògún Alápatà as "Ogun the butcher" in Yorùbá sources, but he owns the knife's edge in every manifestation. Pointing out that, in Lucumí, "the iron deity's vessel is the iron cooking pot containing seven iron tools, an anvil, and a stone," Candice Goucher (2014: 114) writes,

> The Candomble priestess Mainha de Bahia affirms the presence of Ogun in rituals of the kitchen. According to Mainha, prayers to Ogun are said by the female cooks prior to preparing ritual food, and even the manner in which an okra is sliced is particular to Ogun, suggesting that the vocabulary of food was also a form of inscribed ritual.

Oral tradition ties the signature Brazilian pork and black bean stew *feijoada* to Procópio Xavier Souza (1888–1958), leader of the terreiro Ilê Ògúnjà. He is said to have made it for his community one day at Ogum's behest and it caused everyone eating it to "[fall] into trance" (Barton 2018: 293). Not only was it "not a typical feijoada"; apparently this was a *feijoada* with "some ingredients and meats from animals offered to the Ògún of Pai Procopio, the first 'dish' containing certain [sacrificial] flesh that went to the feet of Ògún."[31]

Sacrificial cooking is what has recently been dubbed snout-to-tail cuisine.[32] Among the dishes made for the *orishas*/*orixás* are *eyó* (or *ejó*), cracklings made

---

[31] Babalòrìsà do Terreiro de Òsùmàrè, "A História da Origem da Feijoada de Ògún," January 24, 2016, https://bit.ly/3MV1Jns.

[32] Or "nose to tail cookery," as Barton (2018: 298) puts it.

from fried pork tripe and offered to the Lucumí Olókun. Ogum and Nanã eat Brazilian versions of the Portuguese dish *sarapatel*, a stew of pork or sheep heart, lungs, kidney, liver, and sometimes tripe in a blood sauce. The other *orixá*s have a variation on this dish called *sarrabulho*. Ogum and Oxóssi enjoy *eran peteré*, with beef stomach, tripe, liver, lung, kidney, and minced giblets in red palm oil, onion, smoked shrimp, and castor bean leaves (Eugênio 2002: 42).[33] Kouzen Azaka, the Vodou *lwa* of agriculture, manual labor, and the peasantry, has traditionally received *afibas* (variously described as sun-dried stuffed beef tripe or pork tripe sausage, pan-fried tripe strips, or cured beef tripe that is a type of *tasso*, or jerky) (Bollée et al.: 2017: 6).

Vodouisants use the general term *ofrann* ("offering") to refer to the parts of animals that are removed and set aside for cooking to the *lwa*s' and ancestors' taste (Tudela, Ramos, and Labaut, 2013: 46).[34] Among Candomblé practitioners, "the blood and the vital organs (heart, lungs, liver, kidneys, spleen, etc.)" are called *axés*, with reference to the primordial energy (*axé*) embodied by the deities and their consecrated substances (Motta 2005: 295). Similarly, in Lucumí, the internal organs and other pieces of sacrificial meat reserved for the deities are *achéses*, *ashés*, or *iñales*. The crop, intestines, and cloaca of fowl are extracted and usually discarded, while the analogous parts of "four legs" (along with certain parts of the stomach) have historically been presented to the deities. In Candomblé and Lucumí, the ideal order in which these portions are displayed to the *orishas/ orixá*s (and in conjunction with what words and gestures) have been recorded in notebooks meant for private use among initiates as well as in published manuals.

For example, in a diagram entitled *Manera de presentar la carne* (*Method of Presenting the Meat*) from Cuban Lucumí priest Jesús Torregosa's circa 1936 *libreta*, he identifies "el estómago chico" as *abañú*, followed by "el estómago grande," *ayábala*, and "the two sides and the stomach": *Ifá otó, Ifá dosi, abañú* (Menéndez 1998: 23). All are represented in the diagram by circles of varying sizes. More recently, Ócha'ni Lele has provided a "thick description" of the Lucumí rite in which these parts and others are introduced to the *orisha*s after butchering. While there is much to be gained by studying the history and symbolism of such presentations, I would turn our attention to the most heavily documented of these offerings, what Torregosa lists as *Ochaéroo [or] alaa* and translates into the Spanish term "Redaños" (Menéndez 1998: 23).[35] It is the translucent fatty tissue layer called the omentum or "folds of peritoneum" that hang like a curtain from the abdomen and cover the stomach, liver, kidneys, and other organs.

---

[33] Costa (2017: 250) discusses the composition of this dish in the *panela do fato* ("pan of animal viscera").

[34] Personal communication, Dr. Eziaku Nwokocha, August 20, 2021.

[35] Cabrera (1980: 171) defines *Ochareo alaá* as "redaños" of ram specifically.

Lucumí and Candomblé are far from the only traditions in which the omentum has occupied an exalted place:

> The sacrificial fat referred to [in Hesiod's *Theogony*] and in many Greek texts is the *omentum* (*epipolaion* or *epiploon*), a membrane of suet or lard (depending on the animal) that covers the stomach and intestines. By being offered this fatty substance, the gods were "being given the stuff of life." (Forth 2019: 24–5)

This description rests on the widespread appraisal of this fat as nutritious and appetizing. The omentum was immolated in ancient Jewish, Iranian Zoroastrian, and Hindu Vedic sacrifice and treated differently than other sacrificial portions – for example, it was extracted first, and became a component of some oracles (Knipe 2015: 216). There is a vast literature that expounds upon the meanings and theological implications of the omentum, given the 3,700-year-old history of Vedic sacrifice as prescribed in the Rigveda (composed ca. 1500–1000 BCE), performed even today in Andhra Pradesh, on India's central-southeastern coast. Relying on older analyses, Ganesh Umakant Thite (1970: 145–6) writes, "Not only is the sacrificer regenerated by means of the omentum-offering in the animal-sacrifice ... he is also [said] to obtain immortality." Such readings hinge on the identification of the sacrificial animal with the sacrificer; the fate of the two are intertwined. Those familiar with Black Atlantic traditions might see a family resemblance between the symbolism of the omentum as regeneration – especially when offered in the course of initiatory ritual – and the notion that its offering assists in securing new life for the person responsible for the sacrifice.

For more than a century, the greater omentum has been referred to as "the abdominal policeman" in medical texts. When Rutherford Morison (1906: 76–8) coined the term, he asserted, "There can be no doubt that it travels about in the abdomen with considerable rapidity, and is attracted by some sort of information to neighbourhoods in which mischief is brewing." Morison's image of the omentum as motivated by a will to knowledge hearkens back to sacrificial customs and the role played by the omentum in haruspicy (divination through the inspection of entrails) in ancient Egypt, Mesopotamia, and Rome (Craik 1998). To highlight the omentum's initiative in fighting infection and inflammation, Morison couched these tasks in terms his classically trained colleagues could appreciate. Among surgeons today, "many have not considered it as anything more than a passive, inert, or even vestigial organ that 'gets in the way' or forms troublesome intraperitoneal adhesions" (Bass, Seamon, and Schwab 2020: e161). However, there has been a revival of interest in the omentum's promotion of abdominal healing.

With these qualities in mind, we may perhaps have a better grasp of its importance in Candomblé and Lucumí. Although we cannot presume to know the reasons for its prominence, ethnographic and instructional texts are certainly suggestive. In Lucumí rituals, the omentum is exhibited not only to the *orisha*s in the formal "presentation of meats," but also to everyone within a house of worship, both initiated and uninitiated. For every four-legged animal sacrificed during an initiatory slaughter (*matanzas*), a priest is tasked with walking from room to room, holding up the delicate membrane before the face of each person present while singing the word *"Alachirere!"* Those seeing it are supposed to respond, *"Alá alachirere!"* During my own fieldwork, I have witnessed a variety of reactions to the sight. One night, when a newcomer to the post-sacrificial plucking circle wondered aloud what the *"Alá alachirere"* exchange of speech and glances meant, the ordained elder in charge explained that this membrane is part of the goat's stomach and that in chanting *"Alá alachirere"* one prays for clarity of vision. She then recited a lyric from a praise song for Oshún: *"Alade ko'ju alachirere, Osun alachirere o maa."*[36] In the interest of maintaining ritual secrecy, the correlation between the goat's interior and human sight was not laid bare. The sensitive question nonetheless allowed this senior practitioner to hazard a connection between superficially separate spheres of ritual practice.

This interpretation corresponds to that of others who construe the gesture as being performed "to improve the spiritual vision" (Fichte 1985: 296). Ócha'ni Lele (2012: 154) translates *Alá alachirere* as "The veil brings well-being (iré)" and ties its utterance to a divination verse:

> This part of the ceremony is a custom born of the odu Irosun Meji (4–4). When he walked the earth as a mortal, the man who came to be known as the odu Irosun was clueless; he lived with a self-imposed veil over his eyes ... This ebó [or sacrifice], staring through the abdominal veil, was the ebó that restored his sight. We do this ebó for the same reason ... [Offering the omentum to the *orisha*] is done as a symbolic prayer so the initiates gathered do not find themselves in the same position as the animal just sacrificed – eyes open but unable to see.

This reading of Irosun Meji agrees with an interpretation recorded in my fieldnotes: "[An elder] came through with [the] *Alachirere*. She said that showing it means the animal really is dead, because it's the membrane that holds its intestines in. To look through it is to bear witness. This is important because, she said very clearly, 'We need him,' meaning that his sacrifice mediates between us and the orishas."[37]

Other sources underscore the omentum's power of concealment and fortification.[38] John Mason (1992: 349) translates *"alachirere"* to mean "White

---

[36] Personal communication, April 27, 2007.     [37] Personal communication, November 6, 2005.

[38] These interpretations echo many proverbs such as "One house obscures another; the roof conceals the ceiling; a thin layer of skin covers the stomach, making it impossible to see inside the evildoer" (Owomoyela 2008: 397).

cloth [that] uncover[s] goodness." The omentum has been called an "apron," "fat caul," "fat netting," or "lace fat," keeping the guts together and securing them in the same way an article of clothing shields the body (Onians 1951: 484). In texts pitched to Spanish-speaking Lucumí practitioners, the omentum has sometimes been translated as *abrigo del estomago*, "the jacket of the stomach." In one account of Candomblé practice,

> [T]he animal parts, once prepared, are placed in a wooden or ceramic container and thereafter wrapped with tissue from the nanny-goat's … stomach (called *Axó*, literally meaning "Axe's clothes"). *Axó* prevents negative energy from other undesired entities entering the offering and draining its vitality. The offering is subsequently placed at the "saint's feet," which means in the place devoted to each *orisha*, called "*assentamento*" or "*Ibá* [calabash]."
>
> (Neto, Brooks, and Alves 2009: 4)[39]

A further shade of meaning may be layered onto these. One Ifá diviner asserts that, to comprehend the pronouncement *Alá Alachirere* and the omentum's display, "it is necessary to know an Ifá odun [divination sign] that indicates to the believer that he must always believe what Orula [the patron *orisha* of the Ifá oracle] says because Orula always tells the truth" (Sánchez 1978: 87). Such religious discourses never spell out the exact relationship between vision, recognition, defense, attire, and truth-telling, as though the omentum's real weight has to be felt to be known.[40]

## 6 Strong Stomachs

> I want slaves in our colonies. Liberty is a food for which the stomachs of the negroes are not yet prepared. We must seize any occasion to give them back their natural food, except for the seasonings required by justice and humanity
>
> *(quoted in Dubois 2004: 285).*

So wrote Napoleon Bonaparte's colonial minister, Denis Decrès, advocating the restoration of slavery to Guadeloupe in 1802 after an insurrection on the island inspired by the Haitian Revolution. It is one of the ironies of history that this

---

[39] These membranes appear to be featured in a photograph by Marcello Vitorino, captioned "A young [Candomblé] practitioner prepares for the party near a wall decorated with sacrificed animal skin and entrails. The animals were ritualistically sacrificed the day before and will be served at the party." Lulu Garcia-Navarro, "Brazilian Believers of Hidden Religion Step out of Shadows," *NPR*, September 16, 2013, www.npr.org/sections/parallels/2013/09/16/216890587/brazilian-believers-of-hidden-religion-step-out-of-shadows.

[40] William Bascom ([1951] 1993: 761) recorded the diviner Salako rendering an Odu (Oturupon, 12) that begins,

> "Tortoise enters the forest waddling;
> "The skin that covers the stomach does not let us see the intestines"
> Was the one who cast for Osanyin and Orunmila [Ifa]
> When they were enemies …

same French minister had a hand in the death from starvation of Toussaint Louverture, the formerly enslaved leader of the Haitian independence movement, and in the immiseration of Louverture's wife, Suzanne, the mother of his children (Daut 2020). Casting liberty as an aspirational ideal that is difficult for Others to digest, Decrès infantilized people of African descent as political, moral, and emotional minors not yet ready for solid "food." His appeal to Bonaparte rested on the assumption that freedom takes maturity as well as "guts," both of which Black peoples supposedly had yet to develop. His rhetoric exemplifies the way the alimentary tract has been racialized and mobilized in the service of settler-colonial projects.

In common parlance, to have a "strong stomach" means to be able to eat foods that most people find unpalatable or that are apt to provoke nausea. By extension, it also means to be able to smell, see, hear, or touch unpleasant things without feeling emotionally upset or physically ill. To carry out the type of ritualized disemboweling and dismemberment mentioned in the previous section, one must have a strong stomach by dominant Euro-American standards, bearing in mind the relative rarity of animal slaughter outside of factories or licensed abattoirs. Butchering in religious contexts offends Protestant-normative sensibilities with regard to liturgy as a relatively "bloodless," dispassionate undertaking. I have previously argued that kitchen work inculcates the skills necessary for the intergenerational transmission of Black Atlantic traditions by transforming the corporeal sensoria of practitioners and "seasoning" them into religious competence. Through cooking, they obtain the bodily potentialities that render them capable of feeding the gods and ancestors, thereby ensuring their continued materialization in the world.

Black Atlantic traditions seek to foster strong stomachs through both food preparation and consumption. Rites of passage imbue stomachs with the strength to withstand sensory overload as well as deprivation. In several Afro-Diasporic traditions, the period immediately prior to ordination is one of fasting and feasting, as priests-to-be are alternately restricted in their food intake then compelled to eat and drink things that are strange to them. Practitioners moan about queasiness, heartburn, and irritable bowels in their conversations about initiatory rituals. Some herbs intended to purify the body might clean it out only too well, and not every digestive system can handle meats prepared by ritual cooks according to a combination of lineage-specific precedents and their own idiosyncratic tastes.

Nonetheless, in previous eras, many practitioners would have welcomed eating like gods – like kings and queens – that is, more meat and generally in greater abundance than usual. The archival record beyond the early twentieth century is thin, making it impossible to ascertain whether initiates would have regarded their ritually prescribed diets with fondness or disfavor. The reactions of some (especially in times of food scarcity) might be summed up by the Cuban saying "*Barriga llena, corazón contento*": "Full belly, happy heart."[41] Alfred Métraux (1959: 202) said of Vodou initiates (*ounsis*) in the 1950s:

> They are kept to a rather strict diet which could not exactly be called a fast. Nonetheless they must eat nothing salted. They get nothing but *afibas* (dried tripe) and chicken in the way of meat. Offal (head, feet, gizzards etc.) is particularly reserved for them. The bulk of their diet consists of *gumboes*, *acassan* and maize soup without fats. They only drink water or infusions of *piante* (*Cassia occidentalis*), *corossol* (*Annona muricata*), *bois-dine* (*Eugenia fragans*) or cinnamon.

If Métraux's readers were not aware that offal is a favorite of the deities, they might be tempted to draw a hasty conclusion. Recall Kouzen Zak's *afibas*. By projecting contemporary sensibilities onto practitioners, we miss the extent to which they may have historically derived sensual pleasure and meaningful affective intensity from eating dishes associated with certain deities.[42] And through initiation, practitioners achieve kinship with the gods themselves – a point taken up more fully in the next two sections. For the moment, it may suffice to note that kinship entails kingship – that is, it confers spiritual royalty on initiates.

Initiatory food makes for strong stomachs in another sense. Despite the overwhelming scholarly emphasis on metaphors of consanguineal descent and affinity in Black Atlantic religions, kinship among practitioners across a range of these traditions is also accomplished by eating together (commensality), eating alike (consuming shared substances), observing dietary taboos, and preparing food offerings for the gods and ancestors. Special foods are meant to nurture and strengthen the most vulnerable areas of initiates' physical bodies, even as they suffer a ritual death in the transition from uninitiated practitioner to ordained priest. Initiation itself is frequently viewed as a sacrifice, exchanging the lives of the animals "owned" by the gods for the life of the priest-to-be. Karen E. Richman (2005: 143–4) persuasively casts the Haitian Kanzo initiation ritual as "a sacrificial rite":

> Like the half-starved bull who has been symbolically turned into a splendid offering to the gods, cold, frail, "dried out" (*shèsh*) women are ritually

---

[41] This saying is also popular in other Caribbean and Latin American countries.

[42] The perception of tripe as a delicacy is corroborated by the famous line from Haitian poet Émile Roumer's *Marabout de mon coeur*, "You are the slice of tripe within my gumbo soup" (Stevens 1995: 76). Marie-José Nzengou-Tayo (2007: 175–8) writes, "[A]fter so many years, I am yet to see afiba ('tripe') with calalou ('okra'). Maybe it never existed … maybe it was a figment of Roumer's imagination."

transformed into "hot," "healthy," and "plump" ounsi [initiate]. If, at the annual rite, the descent group sacrifices the life of the bull to the "hungry" *lwa*, at the kanzo they offer the fidelity of ounsi to Danbala and the rest of the "foreign" (*blan*) or "vodou" *lwa* ... These "alien" *lwa* paradoxically validate "the family's" rights (and use of discipline) over their future offspring.

Not coincidentally, the idiom of cooking is taken up with reference to the ritual fortification and disciplining of initiates. A portion of the Kanzo called *boule zen* (the burning of the pots)" involves the application of scalding-hot dumplings to the left hand and foot (Brown 1991: 351). "When this ceremony is completed," Karen McCarthy Brown (2001: 56) observed, "the initiates are told: 'Now you are kwit [cooked]; no one can eat you,' that is to say, no one can do harm to you."

The symbolism of the initiate as both cooked for the gods and kept from existential "spoilage" through heating may be further amplified. Afro-Diasporic religions prize bodies that can hold and transmit the gods' energy in spirit possession as a service to their communities. Similarly, several West and Central African cultures demand that rulers' bodies encompass ancestral and sacred power for the benefit of their subjects. Suzanne Preston Blier (2015: 170) writes, "[In Cameroon], as in Ife, rituals of enthronement also involve acts that serve symbolically to 'cook the king' (make him sacrosanct) similar to the function of a pot." Their container-like bodies are forged partly through ritual-ized food consumption during rites of investiture (Warnier 2007). Anthropologist Johannes Fabian (1990: 65) first heard the Luba-Shaba proverb "Power is eaten whole" when he hesitated to eat a chicken gizzard – "a choice piece because it symbolizes wholeness" – offered to him as an honored guest at a meal among his Congolese interlocutors.

For their bodies to become durable and resilient repositories, practitioners of Black Atlantic traditions must commit to obeying oracular mandates, among which are food taboos and the ingestion of valued substances. These taboos may appear to abide by the classic principles of imitative and contagious magic, but food taboos are not always a matter of "like attracts like," of an effect resem-bling its cause. Although spicy food might be forbidden to a "hot-headed" person in order to promote a "cool" disposition, it might also be disallowed simply due to its connection with a particular deity or divination sign received by that person. Certain foods are proscribed or prescribed according to what will give an individual the strong stomach they need to become a receptacle for divine power.

It is little wonder, then, that practitioners extol the strong stomachs – the high tolerance for extreme discomfort – of those who established African traditions in the Americas. But practitioners of Afro-Cuban *orisha* worship have credited their religious ancestors' stomachs with founding the tradition in quite a literal way. "A common mode of explaining the origins of regla de ocha" is to say that Africans seized by enslavers ingested their most precious consecrated objects, smuggled them onto slave ships in their alimentary tracts, and transported them to the Caribbean in their guts (Palmié 2018: 790n7).[43] For example,

> [O]ne powerful story … relates that, just prior to his capture by slave traders in Africa, the young Adechina "swallowed his Ifá" [sixteen sacred palm nut kernels] … which he carried in his stomach, defecated and guarded in the belly of the slaveship, and later reconsecrated in Cuba. (Brown 2003: 77)

One of the first Ifá diviners on Cuban soil, Ño Remigio Herrera (ca. 1811–1905), is known by his priestly name, Adechina. He was photographed toward the end of his life with the Yorùbá scarification he received as a child visible on his right cheek (Figure 2). David H. Brown (2003: 77) notes that William Bascom collected stories in late 1940s Cuba claiming that the *otánes*, or sacred stones, of Lucumí lineage founders "were 'swallowed' by the slaves prior to their embarcation for the New World," just as Adechina had ingested his Ifá.

In these narratives, the religious ancestors' virtue hinges on their ability to maintain the sacred power concentrated inside their bodies and release it at the perfect moment. They turn their bodies into pots for the *orisha*s in a manner directly analogous to possession mounts' transformation into receptacles for the deities.[44] In analyzing these stories, Brown hews closely to the theme of parturition, which has been salient in Lucumí discourses. In Black Atlantic traditions throughout the Americas, members of a religious community see themselves as part of a family. Biological procreation is central to the symbolism of Lucumí initiation since godparents "give birth" to the *orisha*s of their godchildren in the weeklong ordination ritual of *kariocha* – and to the initiates themselves after they have undergone ceremonial death in the most liminal stage of this rite of passage.[45] Thereafter, initiates shoulder the responsibility of periodically nourishing their own otánes – housed in lidded wooden bowls (*bateas*), porcelain soup tureens (*soperas*), and ceramic jars (*tinajas*) – as well as their physical heads with cooling substances (such as cocoa butter and eggshell chalk), herbal infusions, and sacrifices (*ebó eje*).

---

[43] Lele (2001: 2) included this story in a book but later repudiated it in a Facebook post, July 24, 2019, www.facebook.com/ochani.lele/posts/10217257377080908.

[44] Matory (1994) is perhaps the first to have called attention to this Yorùbá-Atlantic "receptacular" logic and metaphoricity.

[45] In the *kariocha*, the patron deities materialize in the novice's *otánes* and consecrated *otánes* are placed on the crown of the novice's ritually shaved scalp to revive the body that was divested of social being the previous evening (Palmié 2018).

**Figure 2** Remigio Herrera, "Adechina," *Ibae.*

The presence of previously consecrated objects is needed to sacralize others and to ordain priests, who are addressed as the "owners" or "mothers" and "fathers" of the *orisha*s.[46] This process is considered a birthing, regardless of the sex and gender of the senior initiates going through labor (so to speak), or of the *orisha*s being "born" as a consequence. Brown (2003: 77) enhances our appreciation of stories about the ancestors by rendering their subtext explicit: that their stomachs performed a quasi-uterine function and the conservation of sacred objects in the Middle Passage was a type of spiritual pregnancy:

> The clear-thinking, strategic response of swallowing [these foundational objects] in the nick of time required great resourcefulness and prescience on the part of these African ancestors … [U]sing the trope of procreation, the stories then transform the personages of Lucumí ancestors, such as Adechina, into the loving and committed progenitors of tradition. The original Lucumí [foundational objects], the [palm nut kernel] and the [stones], were re-gestated in the stomach of the slave in the belly of the slaveship; in

---

[46] One elder is designated as the primary godparent while the other serves as the *ojugbona* or *yubonna*. Either or both may be male, female, or gender nonbinary/nonconforming.

turn, the body of the ancestor who conserved the[se] precious [objects] was the womb of sacred diasporic tradition.

Notwithstanding the poignancy of Brown's analysis, there is more than can be said about the alimentary tract as a container that does not rest on a reproductive model.

Before arriving at an alternate yet complementary interpretation, it may be useful to consider Stephan Palmié's (2018) overview of Bascom's account:

> As a woman named Florencia Baró told [William Bascom] in August 1948, the stones active in mid-twentieth-century Jovellanos had a history:
>> There was a Lucumi who came here from Guinea as a slave, and swallowed his stones … and brought them here in his stomach. That is how the other Lucumis had stones from these two stones. He died and he gave the stone to another Lucumi, and to another and to another. This is the biggest house [i.e., cult group] in Jovellanos. The Lucumi was a slave of the ingenio Luisa owned by Luisa Baro. All of the slaves were relatives and he founded the religion, her [Florencia's] family came from there. This man had even the little babies [initiated] as soon as they were born; washed their heads [i.e., initiated them] … All the slaves at ingenio [sugar mill] Luisa were ahijados [ritual kin] of this Lucumi, Casimiro Lucumi.

Bascom's story focuses on *otánes*, the stones in which the powers of the *orisha*s reside. Although at the time of this writing Florencia herself would have just been initiated, she knew the "deep folklore" about the stones having been gulped down at just the right moment. She understood that their multiplication through ritual had enlarged the religious families of enslaved people so that the *orisha*s had survived their owners and continued "giving birth" to priests for generations (García 2014: 1–33).

The story also interests us because Casimiro Lucumi could be the very individual so named who was implicated in the Conspiracy of La Escalera in 1843. Aisha K. Finch (2015: 76) writes, "black laborers were drawn into a rebel movement through their work across plantations. Such was the case on the Dos Felices sugar mill in Alacranes – better known as the Mesa property – and the mill adjoining it." Enslaved by Don Manuel Pérez, one "Casimiro [Lucumí] was the main rebel organizer on the Mesa property [Dos Felices]" (Finch 2015: 265n56, 76). "La Luisa" was one of the sugar mills whose fields burned during the rebellion, and it was close enough to Dos Felices that Casimiro might have alternated between the two. Finch (2015: 172) mentions "leaders who were recruited by other slave organizers from nearby plantations," noting that "Many stories surfaced of zealous lieutenants such as Casimiro Lucumí, who appointed two acquaintances on a nearby sugar estate to be captains there." It may also be the case that Florencia misremembered the mill to which Casimiro Lucumí pertained. Or – if Florencia was correct about his enslavement at La Luisa – Casimiro may have been transferred there after serving his ten-year prison sentence, having confessed to gathering weapons for the uprising and fomenting it.[47]

That is not to say that Casimiro Lucumí of Jovellanos must have been Casimiro Lucumí the rebel. Casimiro Lucumí was not an uncommon name in Cuba; there was a second person identified as Casimiro Lucumí, enslaved by Don Francisco de la Luz Caballero, among the rebels of La Escalera who also received a ten-year sentence for the uprising (Cuba 1844). Although we lack the details to flesh out the biography of Casimiro Lucumí, the possibility that he had a role in the Conspiracy of 1843 means that there is more to the story of his stomach than meets the eye. Miguel W. Ramos (2013: 193) has documented the live conviction that Adechina was also "linked with" it: "Oral sources have stressed that his *Cabildo de Santa Bárbara* in Simpson, Matanzas, which Adeshina directed at the time, was a meeting place for the conspirators." Given the oblivion into which the Spanish colonial regime wished to cast the memory of Black insurrectionists, Florencia's testimony might have encoded "subjugated knowledge" of Black fugitivity and resistance.[48] Such recollections may be tied to counter-memories of revolt that subverted official historical accounts and attempted to un-"silence" the Afro-Cuban past (Trouillot 1995).

I submit that stories of stone-swallowing ancestors have acted to dismantle stereotypes, peddled by the likes of Decrès, that classified Black people as too feeble of stomach and mind for liberation. Practitioners of Afro-Cuban religions have celebrated forebears who – far from being "yellow-bellied" or "lily-livered" – had the guts to stand up to the colonial slaveholding regime (Ramos 2013: 73). In the mid-twentieth century, practitioners of Kongo-inspired Palo Monte Mayombe remembered the revolts "in 1843 that cost many slave lives, such as the riots in the *ingenio* Alcancía, of Peñalver, in Cárdenas [and] those of the [Triunvirato] in which the Negroes looted the neighboring ranches and set fire to the sugar plantations, like those of Luisa de Baró" (Lydia Cabrera, quoted in Fhunsu 2017: 150). Cabrera noted of her interlocutors, "For those descendants of the Kongo, it was a title of nobility to declare that their ... foreparents were from the *ingenio* Desengaño ... Triunvirato, San Cayetano, Luisa or Armonía" (quoted in Fhunsu 2017: 67). Practitioners have also paid homage to priests involved in the "Aponte Conspiracy of 1812," whose putative leader, José Antonio Aponte y Ulabarra,

---

[47] Another possibility is that Bascom misunderstood or mistranscribed Florencia's words.

[48] According to Tina Campt, "fugitivity is the 'refusal of the very premises that have historically negated the lived experience of [B]lackness as either pathological or exceptional to white supremacy'" (quoted in von Gleich 2015: 8).

was a veteran of Havana's free Black militia as well as a carpenter and artist. He was reputed to be the head of the aforementioned Cabildo de Santa Bárbara, one of the legendary Lucumí religious societies that became vital incubators for *orisha* worship.

At the very least, the persistence of stories about ancestors like Casimiro Lucumí and Adechina indicates a fervent desire to remember the establishment of *orisha* worship in Cuba as an oppositional act, whether lineage founders took up arms in revolt or not. While this might be a fruitful avenue for future research, West African precedents may provide another means of interpreting the story of Adechina and his Ifá. We might begin with one Yorùbá legend about the patron *orisha* of Ifá divination, Orunmila, being rescued by his favorite wife, Agere: "Once, when Orunmila's enemies were about to catch him, Agere hid her husband inside her stomach to save him" (Drewal 1987: 139–56). This narrative serves to explain why the palm nuts used for divining for clients must be stored in a container called *àgéré Ifá* made of "female wood" and prepared with special medicines, bearing in mind their embodiment of Orunmila's sacred energy. Yet it is also an example of "deep folklore" connected to Ifá diviners that celebrates the swift concealment of their implements in the stomach as a heroic deed.

It is impossible to know whether this legend was in circulation in the nineteenth century to the extent it could have contributed to the way that Adechina was remembered. Contemporary Nigerian discourses may not have any connection with or bearing on the Afro-Diasporic past. But it is intriguing to consider the unique properties and constitution of the Ifá diviner's stomach, according to Yorùbá ritual specialists. Drawing on extensive observant participation and auto-ethnographic research, Amy Harriet Gardner (2010: 1–2) writes,

> Gradually, with experience and practice, the healer-priest/ess is able to consciously direct aspects of Divine Presence-as-healing-force for the thera-peutic benefit of others. Finally, after years of daily scholarly-devotional practice, these musical-embodied practices are refined and body forth a special – sonic and incorporative – somatic mode of being-in and attend-ing-to-the-world particular to Ifá, known as "a stomach as deep as a calabash" (*inú t'ójìnlèbi igbá*), in which Divine Presence is incorporated, as co-pres-ence, within the corporeality and being-in-the-world of the healer-sage.

It would take more space than can be given in this Element to unpack "a stomach as deep as a calabash," starting with the calabash (a hollowed-out dried bottle gourd) as a gendered model of the cosmos itself; the bottom half, analogized to a womb, "represents femaleness," and the top, maleness (Lawal 2008). Like the *àgéré*, the calabash is used to store sacred substances, both in continental Africa and in the African Diaspora, and to fashion rattles and other percussion instruments to be played in ritual contexts.

I would like to dwell for a moment longer on Gardner's rendering of a capacious pot-like stomach as the outcome of an intense sensorily and affectively taxing "scholarly-devotional" process. Gardner (2010: 69n230) relies on fieldwork and etymology to parse the association of the stomach with cognition and affect: "Deep thought as well as pensive reflection, of emotions or thoughts, is referred to as *ìrònú*, literally, 'the stirring [and/or thinking] inside [one's stomach].'" Gardner (2010: 89n295) adds, "The Yorùbá phrase [*ogbón ríbí-ríbí nínú*] implies that deep wisdom is a capacity that is cultivated *nínú* – within the individual's stomach, womb, 'insides.'" Sagacity and receptivity to the indwelling of divine energy proceed from harmonization of the head (*orí*), the "heart-mind" (*okòn*), and "the *inú*, the 'abdomen' and 'insides' (here referring to the corporeal and energetic core as well as to a state of deep – affective and transcendent – interiority)" (Gardner 2010: 125). Gardner ties this matrix of ideas to bodily disciplines such as prostration. The pit of the belly registers the labor done on a daily basis to deepen, expand, and otherwise condition the stomach into a vehicle for optimal mentation.

As in Black Atlantic traditions, illness and affliction are narrated as pivotal moments in the career of many a Yorùbá "healer-priest/ess":

> Corporeal crises are also often a dimension of the healer's individual and on-going process of *attunement* as an instrument of musical performativity as/ and therapeutic power. [They] are fundamental to the formation of the "deep stomach" – *inú t'ójìnlèbi igbá*, literally "a stomach as deep as a calabash" – a referent to the expansive mastery and profound healing power achieved by a small cohort of elder-sages in Ifá. (Gardner 2010: 5–6; italics in the original)

Building tentatively upon Gardner's rich analysis, I would posit that, in stories about Adechina's swallowed Ifá, enslavement occupies the role of corporeal crisis that deepens his stomach. The claim that he conveyed his Ifá across the Atlantic in his belly may have originally signaled the profundity of his extraordinary life to other African-born initiates, then – over time – shed nuances that depended on immersion in the Yorùbá cultural and linguistic context. Adechina's reputation as an elder-sage was earned through not only his thriving divinatory practice and mentorship of younger diviners, but also through his promotion of Lucumí religiosity through the Cabildo de Santa Bárbara and Cabildo de Yemayá, his sponsorship of the second set of consecrated *batá* drums to be reconstructed in Cuba, and his "expansionist campaign" to extend the reach of Egbado traditions and Ifá divination throughout the island (Ramos 2013: 537). Despite the displacement of the stomach by the head (*orí*) in Ifá-centric scholarly discourses, the legacy of Adechina's *inú* continues to reverberate.

## 7 Intestinal Fortitude

This tale burns like hot peppers. But History's not just a tale, History's a bunch of **whys** that stir up a society's guts.

*Michel-Rolph Trouillot (2021: 86)*

If the notion of a "strong stomach" has implied exceptional hardiness and powers of endurance, "intestinal fortitude" conjures the admirable qualities of grit, daring, and determination. Although it has been dismissed as an "infantile phrase" that renders any statement "instantly laughable," its consistent usage since its coinage in the 1860s proves that this euphemism for "guts" fills a discursive niche (Fiske 2006: 20, 191).[49] "Intestinal fortitude" literalizes the corporeality of valor in an instructive way. As one commentator put it in an online linguistics and etymology forum,

> "[G]uts" is a reference to the intestines, which run from the pylorus (at the end of the stomach) to the anus, and "guts" also is a euphemism for "toughness" or "courage."
>
> The phrase "intestinal fortitude" takes this one step further, with implications of tenacity and toughness under fire … Someone with "intestinal fortitude" has mastered their fear instinct AND their sphincter, and when the going gets tough, they have the self control to override their animal instinct to [soil] themselves and run away, and so can stand their ground and prevail.[50]

"Intestinal fortitude" restores to the gut its anatomical particularity as a site generative of emotion, affect, and agency.

The previous section examined the ceremonial efforts to equip Afro-Diasporic religious initiates with strong stomachs and the commemoration of ancestors with enough strength in their stomachs to battle a colonial regime while birthing entire religious lineages. Intestines are a no less racially loaded object of discursive and ritual elaboration. Many cultures associate bravery with the "insides" – no guts, no glory, as the saying goes – and having the confidence to be bold is racially unmarked more often than not, at least in linguistic terms. One exception is Brazilian Portuguese, in which having the "nerve" to do something means *ter raça*, literally, "to have race":

> [T]he question of race, one way or another, has always been fundamentally important in identifying Brazilian national identity … We often use expressions such as "*esse é um sujeito de raça*" (he's got guts), or "*vai com raça*" (go for it), which prove that the term *raça* is by no means neutral. (Schwarcz 2003: 4)

---

[49] "Gastro-intestinal fortitude" appeared in print for the first time to denote "strong stomach," in the sense of a robust digestive system (Fulton 1898: 43).

[50] Cynthia Schletzbaum Gee, "Connotation of 'intestinal fortitude,'" *English Language & Usage*, August 18, 2011, https://bit.ly/3VS6ySv.

The positive association of race with audacity and bravery (as in the adjective *raçudo*) followed centuries of negative connotations (da Silva 2018: 18). It was only after the Iberian ideology of "purity of blood" had loosened its grip that guts and Blackness could become synonymous (Mattos 2008: 22–3).

Cooking in Afro-Diasporic religions involves guts of both kinds, and practitioners have frequently been socialized into communities through it. In my fieldwork in the United States, I found that practitioners' exposure to "variety meats" usually began in the post-sacrificial cooking context, in the early stages of their affiliation with a house of worship. In the Caribbean and Latin America, children may start handling entrails while assisting caregivers in ordinary domestic labor. Scott Alves Barton (2012: 149–50) cites an interview with one elderly Candomblé priestess whose experience mirrored that of several other elderly women who "all told a similar tale of making *galinha à cabidela* (a chicken dish made with its own blood as a sauce)":

> My mother and my grandmother; they brought us into the kitchen as if it was a kind of game when I was a girl. Me and my sister ... I was eight or ten [years old] ... We had to clean and prepare the hen's guts. Yes, the guts. We saved all of the blood. We washed the intestines several times. Then we add seasonings, spices, flour, salt; everything we were told to do. We cooked and ate it ... Yes, I taught my daughter the same way that I learned.

Such cooking has served as a mode of enskillment that habituates girls and femmes into the labor expected of cisgender women and gay men on behalf of the *orixás*.[51]

In Candomblé and other Black Atlantic traditions, "women's work" with entrails has dovetailed with racialized religious labor. As Alberto Heráclito Ferreira Filho (1994: 440) writes,

> Candomblé legitimized female work as it prescribed various earning activities as a way for the "daughters of the saints" to raise money for the fulfillment of their ritual obligations. According to the orixá, the activity varied. Thus, the daughters of Iansà and Xangô sold *acarajé*, those of Ogum, ox viscera.

The traditional Brazilian occupation of *fateira* combined that of cattle, sheep, and pig butcher and market woman (Ferreira 2016: 102; da Silva Paim 2005: 83).[52] Most *fateiras* were Black women and they often had connections to

---

[51] The gendered protocols of Candomblé sacred cooking are similar but not identical to Lucumí's. Capponi (2018: 184) specifies, "While the skinning of the goat is performed by men, its stomach and its intestines need to be cleaned by a woman, preferably a daughter of Oxum or Yansà."

[52] In Cuba, those who "lived by the purchase, cleaning, and sale of beef mondongo, intestines, and bones" were apparently also cisgender Black women (both enslaved and free) called *mondonguera*, *huesera*, *tripicallera*, or *tripera* (Ortiz 1923: 189).

Candomblé houses and religious brotherhoods, such as the famous mid-nine-teenth-century priestess Marcolina da Cidade de Palha, who initiated the afore-mentioned Procópio Xavier Souza as the first cisgender male possession priest (*elegun*) in Bahia (Lessa 2019: 3).

Religious butchering and cooking involve doing what needs to be done, whether you like it or not. This is the meaning of the Spanish idiom *hacer de tripas corazón*, literally, "To make [a] heart of one's guts": to "put on a brave face" and keep going.[53] One does not seek "to pluck up one's courage" for work one wants to do, but for the type of unfree labor that hearkens back to the *senzala*, "the slave quarters" (Harding 2006: 14–15). Practitioners push them-selves physically and exert themselves intellectually as they absorb their elders' complex technical instructions and history lessons. The two converge when elders pause to tease out the relationship between ritual protocols and their ancestors' enslavement. Aisha Beliso-De Jesús (2014: 504) explains,

> Initiation rituals require complex religious skills that reference slavery and African-inspired ways of knowing the world. For instance, when discussing the butchering of animals, Obá Bi told me, "It's about precision … When we open [butcher] the four-leggeds [animals], it's in the traditional way. The animals are saving our lives." He then placed his hand around his neck demonstrating how a noose was once put around the necks of slaves as they were hung from trees. "We cut the meat for the *collar* [necklace/noose] so that we won't be hung like the slaves. It's about being Lucumí … And as we eat the meat, it heals our pains. It makes us whole when most of us are not."
>
> The butchering and consuming of the ritually sacrificed animals is under-stood to ward off this terrible fate. Obá Bi, a light-skinned man of mixed black American and Puerto Rican descent, described how embodied actions of being and becoming Lucumí are linked to forms of racial consciousness.

Doing intricate things precisely is thus cast as paying homage to one's religious ancestors.

This representation of "being and becoming Lucumí" is ideal-typical, since there are now communities made up of mostly of non-Latinx Anglo *aborisha*s and non-Black Latinx "santeros" who are unaware of the linkages between the everyday experiences of their religious forebears and the micropractices they are performing. These practitioners might not be conscious of the relationship between racial consciousness and Lucumí butchering, cooking, and eating. Obá Bi's references to the lynching of the enslaved – like those implicated in the aforementioned revolts – exemplify the interlacement of distinct levels of practice. Not every community includes an Obá Bi with the willingness and

---

[53] "What does the Spanish phrase 'Hacer de tripas corazon' translate into and mean in English?" February 18, 2020, https://bit.ly/3gznflk.

knowledge to teach, in a pedagogical register that is affectively moving as well as effective. And not every practitioner feels as he does, that sacrificial meat heals and makes whole, or that sacred food preparation makes the gods and ancestors real.

One of the offerings traditionally given to the *orisha*s has been a braid made out of the cleaned intestines of birds and four-legged animals. Although the braiding process is not widely discussed, there are vestiges of this micropractice in publications pitched to *santero*s, in which its decline becomes emblematic of the decline of tradition itself. The most detailed account comes from Rodolpho Martin, a Cuban priest initiated in 1944 and interviewed by John Mason (1999: 7) in 1988:

> When we cooked the meat of the goats and rams, we would clean out the stomach and the intestines, braid them and cook them with the *àṣẹ (ọ)kàn yáālẹ* (other innards and special body parts of the sacrificed animals). When the intestines were cooked, they were placed on top of the stew along with balls of yam and packets of *ẹ̀ko* (corn porridge cake) in the number required by each *òrìṣà*.

Prior to the Cuban Revolution of 1959, "the intestines were woven and with them braids were made" as a regular feature of post-sacrificial ritualization (Sánchez 2004: 80).

Jorge Luís Sánchez (2004: 80) mentions the braid in an elegiac passage about Cuba in the early 1970s, when revolutionary ardor resulted in the persecution of Lucumí, the *reglas de congo*, and the religious formation of Abakuá:

> Those years, scarcity marked the practice [of Lucumí]; in 1971 the African swine fever practically exterminated these animals; the snapper began to replace the head of the pig in ceremonies for the ancestors … The weaving of the intestines and sending of the ashés to the places where the orishas live stopped.

New York-based Obá-Oriate Daniel Rodriguez Obábí believes that "the braids become a rarity in Cuba" after 1959 due to the "economic disaster" precipitated by the Revolution, resulting in a lack of fresh water for household use. Using water to clean animal intestines came to be seen as a terrible "waste" of a precious resource.[54]

Such factors cannot account for the braid's absence from rituals outside the island. Lydia Cabrera (1974a: 171) wrote of the braid's increasing rarity among US-based practitioners in the early 1970s, blaming the effects of immigration from Cuba:

---

[54] Personal communication, August 9, 2022.

> Speaking of a sacrificial practice that has been abandoned in exile, a Babalawo recently enlightened me about the dangerous consequences that this can have for the health of the Iyawó [or novice]: "The guts of the animal are no longer woven in the sacrifice of the Asiento [initiation]." These were the subject of a long and cumbersome preparatory rite that consisted of emptying, boiling, and braiding them to present them to the Orishas. In that way in all animal sacrifices the intestines, woven like braids, were placed on the tureen of the oricha that was being fed.

Cabrera does not expand on the harms that could come to the new initiate as a result of their omission.

In these accounts, the braid, or *trenza*, is emblematic of authenticity, as well as the strong stomachs of the elders who maintained Lucumí tradition during their own enslavement and the persecution of Afro-Cuban religions. Ironically, perhaps, some of the likeliest precedents for Lucumí's intestinal plait are not African but European, such as the traditional Spanish *Zarajo* from Cuenca, braided sheep's intestines rolled onto a vine branch and broiled, fried, or smoked; the *Embuchados* of La Rioja; and Aragonese *Madejas*. Many different cuisines the world over contain dishes with woven intestines, such as the Nigerian *Ngwongwo* and *Kayan ciki*; Sardinian lamb dish *Sa Trattalia*, which includes the small intestine along with the liver, spleen, heart, and omentum (*sa nappa*); and *Sa Corda* or *Cordula*, made from lamb stomach and tripe.[55] Native Alaskan Iñupiaq and Alutiiq (or Sugpiaq) peoples make seal intestines into sausages, braid them, then boil or dry them for *Qiluryaq*, *Qulivrat*, or *Iŋaluaq*. While the Lucumí braid is distinctive, it is not unique.

And it is not completely gone. Practitioners still braid intestines for initiations in Miami, New York, and elsewhere in the United States (as in Figure 3), as well as in Havana and Caracas. Echoing Sánchez, Francisco A.-Garrett says (2020: 18),

> In the 1970s … The guts of the [four] legs stopped being woven and other rituals that had been done [before initiation] were exchanged for the spiritual mass. Now, in Venezuela, the previously performed ceremonies described in [religious] tracts were rescued even though some Iworós [initiates], for not having gone through them, are in disagreement with them with respect to certain orishas.

While reports of the intestinal braid's demise have been exaggerated, the consensus appears to be that it is not considered mandatory as it once was. In private conversations and on social media, initiates mourn the loss of braiding as a standard procedure and grieve the death of a generation of elders whose knowledge will not survive them. They also criticize other devotees' inability or unwillingness to butcher animals and cook the sacred portions (*iñales*) for the

---

[55] *La Cucina Italiana*, Editorial staff, "Sa Trattalia: You Can Eat Everything from Sardinian Lamb," February 2, 2020, www.lacucinaitaliana.com/italian-food/italian-dishes/sa-trattalia-you-can-eat-everything-from-sardinian-lamb.

**Figure 3** Traditional braids, or *trenzas*, for the *orisha*s depicted in a dried gourd with cooked corn, yam balls, and sacred meat. The photograph was taken by Obá-Oriate Daniel Rodriguez Obábí and is gratefully reproduced with his kind permission.

*orishas*, thereby preventing the transfer of historical information shared by figures like Obá Bi (Ramos 2012: iii).[56]

Their angst is echoed by scholar-practitioner Adonis Sánchez Cervera (2022), who warns that *orisha* worship is deteriorating due to the "commercialization of

---

[56] In 1991, Mercedes Cros Sandoval interviewed Florencio Baró – very likely a descendant or relation of Florencia Baro – and he gave an overview of *orisha* worship in the town of Carlos Rojas, Jovellanos, in the 1940s and 1950s. He emphasized the power of *iñales* to heal when ingested and criticized urban practitioners for disposing of them (which is the most common way of dealing with them today):

> Saints eat the head and the feet of the animals, because without the head and the feet no one can go anywhere. They also eat the viscera ... These *iñales* were offered to the saints for a day. Then they were given to the children. Since children have no bad feelings and have clean hearts, the *iñales*, which are medicinal, were given to them. In Cárdenas, they gave the *iñales* to the children, or they threw them away. In Havana they put them in the trash can.

> (Baró, quoted in Cros Sandoval 2006: 65)

religious goods and services" and outright "charlatanism." Playing on the meanings of "liquid" as both a "fluid" and "cashable asset," Sánchez Cervera (2022) laments,

> We are living a liquid Santería [*santería líquida*], as the babalosha Hermano José points out, which has allowed the elders' wisdom to escape after their deaths; [like] the strength, respect, and ties that were previously established in relations of religious kinship, within the lineages, families, and houses of the saints. Humility, respect, and religiosity are slipping away like water between one's fingers.

The phrase *santería líquida* was coined by Hermano José in a June 2017 Facebook post entitled "The Kitchen," a paean to Lucumí cooks and culinary traditions – such as the preparation of *iñales* – that concludes, "When 'liquid santeria' arrives, one of the first things it does is put an end to the previous customs and among them that of the kitchen." When some communities today dispose of sacrificial remains altogether, how are newcomers to learn the connection between the flesh of the neck and the noose?

Some practitioners forgo the braid along with the ritualized presentation of the meats not due to ignorance but ideological objections. Several of these may be found in an anonymous religious tract, "13 Differences in Worship between Yoruba and Santeria," that seems to have been posted online in April 2003 and disseminated widely beginning in 2007. The author, a "Neotraditionalist" Ifá diviner apparently based in Spain, condemns the elaborate sacrificial protocols of Lucumí communities and recommends dispensing with Afro-Cuban traditions that do not conform to contemporary Nigerian practices.[57] He fulminates,

> There are even many priests of the New World who carry out an act called "presentation of the meats" which consists in the fact that, once the animals that have been slaughtered are dead, they skillfully dismember their bodies while singing joyful songs – depending on the officiant's seriousness – dedicated to the deities …
>
> It does not make any ethical – and much less sacred – sense, to tear off pieces of meat, extract bones, weave guts, remove membranes and guts from the corpses of sacrificed animals and then sing and dance with them or around them (as some do with the heads of the goats and sacrificed sheep), just as the barbarians and other semi-savage ethnic groups used to do with the severed heads of their enemies.[58]

The author goes on to claim that Nigerian Yorùbá sacrifices are swift, nearly silent, and somber affairs with "no macabre dances or liturgical dismemberment,"

---

[57] Entitled, "13 Diferencias de Culto entre el Yoruba y la Santeria" (thereby feminizing Santeria by contrast with the masculine Yoruba), the tract was sold as a book in May 2020 (https://bit.ly/3SrUF2E).

[58] The tract was posted in five distinct chapters (and file downloads) on Yorubaweb ("Ile Awon Balogun") [yorubaweb@lycos.es] in April 2003: https://bit.ly/3TuqEAv.

or "songs when removing parts of the corpses, songs and dances with the animals' heads, songs with the exhibition of certain bloody membranes," and so forth. He assumes that the latter are syncretic impurities that accrued over time as geographical and temporal distance from West Africa increased, rather than precolonial practices that Cubans preserved even as they diminished on the African continent itself, in the shadow of Protestant Christian missionization and Islamicization.

It may seem ironic that this "Neotraditionalist" would echo Willem Bosman's critique of "Eyntjeba." But whether penned by a Nigerian, Cuban, or Venezuelan Ifá diviner (or none of the above), the criticism voiced in the tract rests on conventional Euro-American standards for rationality that leave no room for what appears to be liturgical excess or affective exuberance. It is difficult to estimate the number of practitioners who would espouse this argument, but the attraction to "Neotraditionalist" Nigerianization and "Nagô hegemonization" is only growing in Brazil, just as *yorubización* is among practitioners of Cuban-style *orisha* worship elsewhere. The evidence for the appeal of these re-Africanization movements may be adduced by not only the presence of ideologically aligned communities in "meatspace" (brick-and-mortar houses of worship) but also by the proliferation of publications, websites, and workshops that promise a ritual return to Africa that need not concede anything to the Diasporic past nor insist on the veneration of enslaved religious ancestors.

In October 2009, "13 Differences" inspired a spirited response from the late Cuban-born Ifá diviner Leonel Gámez Céspedes and Águila de Ifá ("eagle of Ifá") called *Defendiendo nuestras tradiciones*.[59] The Cuban-born Gámez Céspedes had moved to Mexico City in 1991 and founded Ilé Ifá Association of Mexico in 2003 (Huet 2013: 178–9). Practitioners sometimes locate rationales for performing rituals a certain way in divination verses, and several sources agree that the presentation of the meats was "born" in the sign Baba Ejiogbe (or Eyeunlé, 8), called "father" or "king" of the divination corpus because it is held to be senior to all the other signs (Bernal [2008] 2010, 63; Mason 1999, 58–9).[60] Gámez Céspedes and Águila de Ifá elected not to cite it, however. In fact, they did not counter the aspersions cast on sacrificial butchering or rituals directly at all.[61] Instead, they (2009: 23–4) related a story in which

---

[59] A third tract was published by (Sociedad Yoruba de México y Águila de Ifá Foundation, January 2012) www.ecured.cu/Leonel_G%C3%A1mez_C%C3%A9spedez. It is possible that the tract grew out of this thread begun by Gámez Céspedes: "Ifá Afrocubano y Ifá Tradicional," July 21, 2009, www.ashe.com.ve/foro/viewtopic.php?t=12153. See also Awo Ifa Ladde, "Quien es Aguila de Ifa," October 2, 2019, www.youtube.com/watch?v=ezRzL7UZ2QA.

[60] Other texts suggest the divination sign Iká Meyi.

[61] On an online forum, Gámez Céspedes had advocated the cooking of *iñales* and spoken out against the post-sacrificial disposal of unbutchered carcasses as the hallmark of charlatans and

Orunmila was told by his own diviner that he had to make an *ebó*, a sacrifice, "and they told him that he had to cook the Iyanles [*iñales*]." This led to Orunmila's eventual triumph over a group of robbers in hot pursuit.[62]

As the leader of the Sociedad Yoruba de México at the time of his death in 2014, Gámez Céspedes knew his audience.[63] He and Águila de Ifá might have intuited that endorsing the weaving of intestines and waving of membranes too loudly might alienate practitioners worried about achieving respectability as members of a stigmatized minority religion. It might reinforce sensationalistic stereotypes of those who "immediately fall upon [a rooster or sheep] and tear it to pieces with their Fingers." More rhetorically convincing to readers would be the invocation of guts in a metaphorical sense:

> It is a criminal attack against an entire culture, trying to smear the work of those who, being outside of their own lands, in someone else's land and also whipped by the lash and who – even so – had the fortitude and the courage to maintain their religion until today. Likewise, it is a criminal attack to try to sully the work of those [continental Africans] who, seeing their land invaded and subjected to foreign governments and cultures, and who – even so – also had the courage and integrity to rescue their beliefs in the best way they were able. This must end. (Gámez Céspedes and Águila de Ifá 2009: 27)

While phenotypically white like many practitioners of Lucumí, Palo Monte, and Candomblé, Gámez Céspedes was highly invested in the memory of religious ancestors who had been enslaved. Their intestinal fortitude would have to be cited in lieu of the labor through which they rescued themselves.

## 8 Spilling (Your) Guts

The kitchen is the gut of the home. It is a site saturated by emotion where food is processed in an expenditure of energy that produces an energy all its own. In Black Atlantic religions, kitchenspaces happen in damp cellars, in the open air, or wherever practitioners can be accommodated (Christie 2008). Sometimes the deities themselves butcher and cook when incorporated by their possession mounts:

---

scammers. "Charlatanes y Estafadores en Mexico," September 26, 2010, www.ashe.com.ve/foro/viewtopic.php?t=18915.

[62] I have been unable to find the exact Odu, which turns on the Muslim identities of Orunmila's antagonists. The context suggests "Odù Otura-Meyi, which in Afro-Cuban tradition is called Ifá Male" (Guerra 2015: 405).

[63] Gámez Céspedes had published one book, was at work on two others, and had cowritten three tracts defending Afro-Cuban *orisha* worship when he was murdered by two assailants in 2014. Three years later, the vice president of the Sociedad Yoruba de México, Daniel Ramírez, was also murdered, which was followed shortly thereafter by the murder of the Sociedad's president, Israel Salazar Sánchez. *Excelsior*, October 9, 2014, www.excelsior.com.mx/comunidad/2014/10/09/985994, Ivan Ramirez, "Israel Salazar Sánchez, el Yoruba que vivía escondido," *Milenio*, June 21, 2018, https://bit.ly/3zazXgX.

Often after a festival is finished, the spirits stay long into the morning, sitting and talking with people. "Jean Dantor loves to sit with people!" Marie Rose told me. In fact, "it's the spirits themselves who show us how to share, it is they who show us how to live" ... Indeed, it was Jean Dantor who sat with us in the sunny, outdoor kitchen supervising how the sacrificed goat's meat was to be divided, prepared, and shared between neighbors, friends, and family. (Sager 2009: 101)

Jean Dantor is one Haitian family's *lwa* who is considered "a member of Ogoun Balendjo's corps of bodyguards." Bearing in mind what we have said about Ogún/Ogum/Ogoun, it is no coincidence that a spirit aligned with him organized their communal meal (Matory 1994: 17; Pérez 2021: 336).[64] His active appearance at the community's core externalized the *lwas*' immanent presence in initiates' bodies.

Kitchenspaces generate countless opportunities for incorporated deities and elders to teach impromptu lessons. As the deities' representatives, ritual cooks play an enormously consequential role in socializing outsiders into religious communities. When they pause to give instruction, the scene resembles the moment captured by photographer Phil Clarke Hill in 2013 (Figure 4) on Calle Luz in Old Havana, in which a beloved elder, Lucia, has commanded the room. Amanda Caroline de Oliveira Pereira (2015: 48–9) writes of one ethnographic interlocutor that, as a child, she got into the habit of cooking a local chicken dish called *cozinhado*:

She and her friends would go to the back door of the *terreiro* [Candomblé community] after school without her mother knowing, and would ask Morena de Omolú, a Iyabassé [ritual cook], for the *tripas* of the chicken which were left over from the sacrifices and dishes made for the *orixás*. The love and care that she received from Morena de Omolú provided her with a significant longing and desire to be an insider of Candomblé and not just a recipient of its resources from the outside.

That child later became a practitioner, with Morena de Omolú serving as an initiatory mentor.

Intergenerational instruction in the kitchen itself involves training practitioners to manage their gut feelings during the post-sacrificial preparation of food. While newcomers and elders prepare meat for sacred meals, they internalize their teachers' aesthetic directives. They start curating their emotions – including those of discomfort and disgust – so as to do the most through job possible of skinning, plucking, rinsing clean, and chopping up sacrificial meat. Joseph Marchal (2019: 117) notes, "Disgust seems automatic

---

[64] Divination verses also portray Elegguá as cooking meat.

**Figure 4** Kitchenspace as commanded by Lucia on Calle Luz in Old Havana, by Phil Clarke Hill, 2013.

and involuntary, especially since it provokes an immediate, physical reaction – revulsion, a gag, a retch, or a sneer. Disgust is not just a feeling, it's a gut feeling." This does not mean that disgust is natural: "disgust is in more than the guts[;] it is mediated and thus must be read" (Marchal 2019: 124; Ahmed [2004] 2014: 83). Elders are experts at deconstructing disgust as the result of hegemonic conditioning. Through speech, physical touch, and visually arrest-ing gestures, they communicate that what might seem revolting today will be routine tomorrow.

In the process of becoming competent religious practitioners, newcomers attain a oneness of purpose with their peers. Engaging in the sensorimotor and affective labor demanded within kitchenspaces, they develop an espirit de corps that comes from doing hard work in close quarters and from laughing at the gallows humors that bubbles up in the wee hours of the morning, when pressure is running high, defenses are low, and verbal filters are nonexistent. The idiom "busting a gut" refers both to toiling strenuously and laughing uproariously, and kitchenspaces ring with belly laughs at the most inappropriate moments. In some ritual settings, laughter can mark the onset of possession, but, in the kitchen, its magic lies in its power to relieve anxieties practitioners have brought with them from outside the house of worship. Laughter releases tensions generated in friction with fellow practitioners too; laughing until it hurts is far preferable to venting one's spleen in anger within elders' earshot.

As spaces marginalized in the discourse on Black Atlantic traditions, kitchenspaces attract marginalized discursive forms. When practitioners cross corporeal boundaries, their emotional vulnerability leads to volubility. Surrounded by sacrificial remains, practitioners' minds turn to their own loss of bodily integrity and ontological security. As they literally gut and spill, they are moved to spill their guts – to share private emotions and divulge sensitive information. Practitioners might not be able to tell confidantes later what they will say to total strangers while butchering and cooking. This play of emotional and material revelation and concealment makes these religious kitchenspaces transformative sites of affectively charged familial intimacy.

Their historical status as such is attested by two Afro-Cuban proverbs: *Al amigo nuevo no se le lleva a la cocina* – "The new friend is not taken to the kitchen" – and *No hay casa sin puerta, y el último secreto está en la cocina* – "There is no house without a door, and the final secret is in the kitchen" (Cabrera 1974b: 372). The word "secret" has a double meaning in religious contexts: it is not only a confidence whispered among old friends, but the "deep knowledge" of how to make ritual action efficacious, like what consecrating the objects that embody the deities entails. Such "deep knowledge" underlies the "hermeneutics of power" that structure interpretive frameworks in Afro-Diasporic religions as well as Yorùbá traditional religion (Apter 1991). John Mason (1999: 62) writes: "Everything that goes on in the igbódù [sacred grove/inner sanctum] is reflected in the kitchen. My teacher, Christopher Oliana ['one of the founding fathers' of *orisha* worship in the United States] advised me, 'If you want to know where they are in the ritual order keep your eyes on the kitchen and your ears open to the songs being sung'" (Thompson 1983: 25)

Among the "open secrets" disclosed in kitchenspaces are elders' initiation stories, in which they depict affliction as a call to priesthood. In the speech genre of "unchosen choice," priests recount the process whereby they learned to decipher medical symptoms and inexplicable accidents as messages from the gods and ancestors (Pérez 2013a). The "open secret" of the initiation story has taught junior members of religious communities crucial lessons about the gods' reality and power. The more uninitiated listeners enter sympathetically into the suffering of priestly narrators, the more they become affectively interwoven with them. This abstract sense of sympathy aroused by the initiation story is canalized into a more concrete application of care in food preparation, when – to properly feed others – it is imperative to inquire into what they can (and cannot) eat. For the uninitiated, memorizing the dietary preferences of both human elders and deities is an act of deference that intensifies their relationships, built partly on revelations made in the kitchen.

Practitioners' intellectual comprehension of themselves as members of a family becomes a gut feeling of common adversity and joint survival. Theirs is a family not of blood (in the sense of biology) but of stone (like the one in Casimiro Lucumí's belly). This mentation of kinship can manifest in the rush of the stomach dropping or a sinking twinge in the gut that weakens the knees. In Black Atlantic traditions, gut feelings naturalize religious kinships that anthropologists once called "fictive"; they legitimate the efforts made to make strong stomachs out of delicate ones and to inculcate intestinal fortitude. They ache with awe at the unfathomable depth of a beloved elder's expertise and they roil with nausea at the unexpected news that that elder has died. While gut feelings can strike when something is amiss, they can signal a positive immediate certainty that a situation is just right – when the beat drops at a club or the drum rhythm breaks at a *bembé*.[65] Gut feelings may even be beings: any number of deities or the dead. To investigate them further would help shake off the hold of the head on religion, and bring it down closer to where the magic really happens.

---

[65] A *bembé* is a Lucumí drum ritual.

# Bibliography

Abiodun, R. (2014). *Yoruba Art and Language: Seeking the African in African Art*. London: Cambridge University Press.

A.-Garrett, F. (2020). *Regla de Osha Afrocubana en Venezuela*. Raleigh, NC: Lulu Press.

Ahmed, S. ([2004] 2014). *The Cultural Politics of Emotion*. Edinburgh: Edinburgh University Press.

(2012). *On Being Included: Racism and Diversity in Institutional Life*. Durham, NC: Duke University Press.

Alpizar, R., and Calleja, G. (2019). *Nfumbe: El universo de los espíritus como lenguaje articulado en el palo monte Mayombe*. Havana: Ediciones Maiombe.

Angarica, N. V. (1955). *Manual del oriaté, religión lucumí*. Havana.

Apter, A. (1991). Herskovits's heritage: Rethinking syncretism in the African Diaspora. *Diaspora*, 1(3), 235–60.

(2018). *Oduduwa's Chain: Locations of Culture in the Yoruba-Atlantic*. Chicago, IL: University of Chicago Press.

Austin-Broos, D. J. (1997). *Jamaica Genesis: Religion and the Politics of Moral Orders*. Chicago, IL: University of Chicago Press.

(2003). The anthropology of conversion: An introduction. In A. Buckser and S. D. Glazier, eds., *The Anthropology of Religious Conversion*. New York: Rowman and Littlefield, pp. 1–14.

Avalos, N. (2018). Decolonial approaches to the study of religion: Teaching Native American and Indigenous religious traditions. *Religious Studies News*, November 5. https://bit.ly/3gzDMG6.

(2020). Interview: Decolonizing religious studies and its layers of complicity, with D. McConeghy, August 17. https://bit.ly/3D1sSAp.

Babatunde, E. D. (1992). *A Critical Study of Bini and Yoruba Value Systems of Nigeria: Change: Culture, Religion, and the Self*. Lewiston, NY: E. Mellen Press.

Balkenhol, M. (2021). Commemorating the African ancestors: Entanglements of citizenship, colonialism, and religion in the Netherlands. In L. Medovoi and E. Bentley, eds., *Religion, Secularism, and Political Belonging*. Durham, NC: Duke University Press, pp. 265–82.

Barton, S. A. (2012). "Can you take a picture of the wind?": Candomblé's absent presence framed through regional foodways and Brazilian popular music. *Canadian Journal of Latin American and Caribbean Studies*, 37 (74), 137–72.

(2018). "Now you're eating slave food!" A genealogy of feijoada, race, and nation. In S. Ickes and B. Reiter, eds., *The Making of Brazil's Black Mecca: Bahia Reconsidered*. East Lansing: Michigan State University Press, pp. 279–306.

Bascom, W. ([1951] 1993). *Sixteen Cowries: Yoruba Divination from Africa to the New World*. Bloomington: Indiana University Press.

Bass, G. A., Seamon, M. J., and Schwab, C. W. (2020). A surgeon's history of the omentum: From omens to patches to immunity. *Journal of Trauma and Acute Care Surgery*, 89(6), e161–e66.

Bayart, J.-F. (1989). *L'État en Afrique. La politique du ventre*. Paris: Fayard.

Begot, D. (1980). Le vaudou dans la peinture. *Espace créole*, 4(1), 99–108.

Beliso-De Jesús, A. M. (2014). Santería copresence and the making of African Diaspora bodies. *Cultural Anthropology*, 29(3), 503–26.

(2015). *Electric Santería: Racial and Sexual Assemblages of Transnational Religion*. New York: Columbia University Press.

Bernal, G. ([2008] 2010). *La dilogmancia "El Oráculo Del Diloggún," La Sagrada Mision de Consultar*. Raleigh, NC: Lulu Press.

Blier, S. P. (1995). Vodun: West African roots of Vodou. In D. J. Cosentino, ed., *Sacred Arts of Haitian Vodou*. Los Angeles: UCLA Fowler Museum, pp. 61–87.

(1996). *African Vodun: Art, Psychology, and Power*. Chicago, IL: University of Chicago Press.

(2015). *Art and Risk in Ancient Yoruba: Ife History, Power, and Identity, c. 1300*. Cambridge: Cambridge University Press.

Bollée, A., Kernbichl, K., Scholz, U., and Wiesinger, E. (2017). *Dictionnaire étymologique des créoles français d'Amérique: Deuxième Partie, Mots d'origine non-française ou inconnue*. Hamburg: Helmut Buske.

Bosman, W. (1705). *A New and Accurate Description of the Coast of Guinea, Divided into the Gold, Slave and Ivory Coasts*. London: J. Knapton, D. Midwinter.

Brown, D. H. (1989). Garden in the machine: Afro-Cuban sacred art and performance in urban New Jersey and New York. PhD dissertation, Yale University.

(2003). *Santería Enthroned: Art, Ritual, and Innovation in an Afro-Cuban Religion*. Chicago, IL: University of Chicago Press.

(2022). *Patakín: Orisha Stories from the Odu of Ifa*. Ocean, NJ: AshéExpress.

Brown, K. M. (1991). *Mama Lola: A Vodou Priestess in Brooklyn*. Berkeley: University of California Press.

(1995). The altar room: A dialogue. With Mama Lola and K. M. Brown. In D. Cosentino, ed., *Sacred Arts of Haitian Vodou*. Los Angeles: UCLA Fowler Museum, pp. 227–39.

(2001). Afro-Caribbean healing: A Haitian case study. In *Healing Cultures: Art and Religion As Curative Practices in the Caribbean and Its Diaspora*, ed. M. Fernández Olmos and L. Paravisini-Gebert. New York: St. Martin's Press, pp. 43–68.

Brown, T. K. (2003). Mystical experiences, American culture, and conversion to Christian Spiritualism. In A. Buckser and S. D. Glazier, eds., *The Anthropology of Religious Conversion*. New York: Rowman and Littlefield, pp. 133–48.

Browse, S. (2018). *Cognitive Rhetoric: The Cognitive Poetics of Political Discourse*. Amsterdam: John Benjamins.

Bruce, L., and Lane Ritchie, S. (2018). The physicalized mind and the gut-brain axis: Taking mental health out of our heads. *Zygon*, 53(2), 356–74.

Burton, R. D. E. (1997). *Afro-Creole: Power, Opposition, and Play in the Caribbean*. Ithaca, NY: Cornell University Press.

Cabrera, L. ([1954] 1968). *El monte: Igbo, finda, ewe orisha, vititi nfinda*. Miami, FL: Ediciones C.R.

([1957] 1986). *Anagó: vocabulario lucumí. El yoruba que se habla en Cuba*. Miami, FL: Ediciones Universal.

(1974a). *Yemayá y Ochún: Kariocha, Iyalorichas y Olorichas*. Madrid: C & R.

(1974b). Oye Ogbó. Refranes y ejemplos. Cómo enseñaban a sus hijos los viejos lucumíes y taitas criollos. In V. Báez, ed., *La Enciclopedia de Cuba. Prosa de guerra. Geografía. Folklore. Educación. Economía*. Vol. 6. Madrid: Enciclopedia y Clásicos Cubanos, pp. 349–82.

Cámara, D. (2009). *El Dilogun, Manual Adivinatorio, La Sabiduria Del Caracol*. Raleigh, NC: Lulu Press.

Capponi, G. (2018). A dialogue with nature: Sacrificial offerings in Candomblé religion. PhD dissertation, University of Roehampton.

Carden-Coyne, A. (2005). American guts and military manhood. In C. E. Forth and A. Carden-Coyne, eds., *Cultures of the Abdomen: Diet, Digestion and Fat in the Modern World*. New York: Palgrave Macmillan, pp. 71–86.

Carr, D. (2003). *Education, Knowledge, and Truth: Beyond the Postmodern Impasse*. London: Routledge.

Cartwright, K. (2013). *Sacral Grooves, Limbo Gateways: Travels in Deep Southern Time, Circum-Caribbean Space, Afro-Creole Authority*. Athens: University of Georgia Press.

Castor, N. F. (2017). *Spiritual Citizenship: Transnational Pathways from Black Power to Ifá in Trinidad*. Durham, NC: Duke University Press.

Chakrabarty, D. (2000). *Provincializing Europe: Postcolonial Thought and Historical Difference*. Princeton, NJ: Princeton University Press.

Chireau, Y. P. (1993). *Black Magic: Religion and the African American Conjuring Tradition*. Berkeley: University of California Press.

Chock, P. P. (1967). Some problems in Ndembu kinship. *Southwestern Journal of Anthropology*, 23(1): 74–89.

Christie, M. E. (2008). *Kitchenspace: Women, Fiestas, and Everyday Life in Central Mexico*. Austin: University of Texas Press.

Condé, M. (1983). Naipaul et les Antilles: Une histoire d'amour? *La Quinzaine littéraire*, 16(31), 6–7.

Costa do Nascimento, M. (2017). Sacrifício de animais e distribuição da carne no ritual afro-pernambucano. In R. Motta, ed., *Os afro-brasileiros: Anais do Congresso Afro-Brasileiro*. Recife: Massangana, pp. 245–52.

Craik, E. M. (1998). *Hippocrates: Places in Man*. Clarendon.

Cros Sandoval, M. (2006). *Worldview, the Orichas, and Santería: Africa to Cuba and Beyond*. Gainesville: University Press of Florida.

Crowther, S. A. (1843). *Vocabulary of the Yoruba Language, Part I. English and Yoruba. Part II. Yoruba and English. To which are Prefixed, the Grammatical Elements of the Yoruba Language*. London: Church Missionary Society.

Cuba, Comisión Militar Ejecutiva y Permanente. (1844). *Colección de los fallos pronunciados por una sección de la Comisión militar establecida en la ciudad de Matanzas para convocer de la causa de conspiración de la gente de color, etc*. Matanzas: Imprenta del gobierno por S. M. y la Real marina.

Daniel, Y. (2005). *Dancing Wisdom: Embodied Knowledge in Haitian Vodou, Cuban Yoruba, and Bahian Candomblé*. Champaign: University of Illinois Press.

Daut, M. L. (2020). The wrongful death of Toussaint Louverture. *History Today*. https://bit.ly/3N4m1uF.

Derrida, J., and Moore, F. C. T. (trans.). (1974). White mythology: Metaphor in the text of philosophy. *New Literary History*, 6(1), 5–74.

Díaz Castrillo, L. (2006). *Manual del Santero II*. Caracas: Inversiones Orunmila.

Dillard, C. B. (2000). The substance of things hoped for, the evidence of things not seen: Examining an endarkened feminist epistemology in educational research and leadership. *Qualitative Studies in Education*, 13(6), 661–81.

Dingemanse, M. (2006). *The Body in Yorùbá: A Linguistic Study*. Leiden: University of Leiden.

Drewal, H. J. (1987). Art and divination among the Yoruba: Design and myth. *Africana Journal*, 14(2–3), 139–56.

Dubois, L. (2004). *Avengers of the New World: The Story of the Haitian Revolution*. Cambridge, MA: Harvard University Press/Belknap Press.

Dukes, D., Abrams, K., Adolphs, R., et al. (2021). The rise of affectivism. *Nature Human Behaviour*, June 10. https://doi.org/10.1038/s41562-021-01130-8.

Ellis, A. B. (1887). *The Tshi-Speaking Peoples of the Slave Coast of West Africa: The Religion, Manners, Customs, Laws, Languages*. London: Chapman and Hall.

(1894). *The Yoruba-Speaking Peoples of the Slave Coast of West Africa: Their Religion, Manners, Customs, Laws, Language, &c.* London: Chapman & Hall.

Emmanuel, A. K. T. (2017). African concept of man and his destiny. www .academia.edu/37179990/AFRICAN_CONCEPT_OF_MAN_AND_ HIS_DESTINY_BY_AJAYI_KEHINDE_TEMITOPE_EMMANUEL. Unpublished paper.

Espírito Santo, D. (2015). Liquid sight, thing-like words, and the precipitation of knowledge substances in Cuban Espiritismo. *Journal of the Royal Anthropological Institute*, 21(3), 579–96.

Eugênio, R. W. (2002). *Acaçá: Onde tudo começou: Histórias, vivências e receitas das cozinhas de Candomblé*. São Paulo: Arx.

Fabian, J. (1990). *Power and Performance: Ethnographic Explorations through Proverbial Wisdom and Theater in Shaba, Zaire*. Madison: University of Wisconsin Press.

Ferreira, E. (2016). O Bumba-Meu-Boi do Piauí: Poesia afro-brasileira, cantigas, gênese, memórias e narrativas de fundação do Boi de Né Preto de Floriano Piauí. *Vozes, Pretérito & Devir*, 6(1), 92–106.

Fichte, H. (1985). *Lazarus und die Waschmaschine: kleine Einführung in die afroamerikanische Kultur*. Frankfurt: Fischer.

Filho, A. H. Ferreira (1994). Salvador das mulheres condição feminina e cotidiano popular na Belle Époque imperfeita. M.A. thesis, Federal University of Bahia.

Finch, A. K. (2015). *Rethinking Slave Rebellion in Cuba: La Escalera and the Insurgencies of 1841–1844*. Chapel Hill: University of North Carolina Press.

Fiske, R. H. 2006. *The Dimwit's Dictionary: More Than 5,000 Overused Words and Phrases and Alternatives to Them*. Portland, OR: Marion Street Press.

Fhunsu, D., trans. (2017). *The Kongo Rule: The Palo Monte Mayombe Wisdom Society (Reglas de Congo: Palo Monte Mayombe*. PhD dissertation, University of North Carolina at Chapel Hill.

Flora, C. (2007). Gut almighty. *Psychology Today*, May 1. www.psychologytoday .com/us/articles/200705/gut-almighty.

Forde, M. (2018). Introduction. In M. Forde and Y. Hume, *Passages and Afterworlds: Anthropological Perspectives on Death in the Caribbean*. Durham, NC: Duke University Press, pp. 1–30.

Forth, C. E. (2019). *Fat: A Cultural History of the Stuff of Life*. London: Reaktion.

Fulton, J. S. (1898). The sanitation of seaside resorts. *Maryland Medical Journal: Medicine and Surgery*, 38, 41–5.

Gámez Céspedes, L., and Águila de Ifá. (2009). *Defendiendo nuestras tradiciones*. www.academia.edu/25470490/Defendiendo_Nuestras_Tradiciones.

García, D. F. (2014). Contesting anthropology's and ethnomusicology's will to power in the field: William R. Bascom's and Richard A. Waterman's fieldwork in Cuba, 1948. *MUSICultures*, 40(2), 1–33.

Gardner, A. H. (2010). Incorporating divine presence, orchestrating medical worlds: Cultivating corporeal capacities of therapeutic power and transcendence in Ifa everyday. PhD dissertation, University of California, Berkeley.

Gibson, K. (2001). *Comfa Religion and Creole Language in a Caribbean Community*. Albany: State University of New York Press.

Giles-Vernick, T. (1999). Leaving a person behind: History, personhood, and struggles over forest resources in the Sangha Basin of Equatorial Africa. *International Journal of African Historical Studies*, 32(2/3), 311–38.

Goucher, C. (2014). Rituals of iron in the Black Atlantic World. In Akinwumi Ogundiran and Paula Saunders, eds., *Materialities of Ritual in the Black Atlantic*. Bloomington: Indiana University Press, pp. 108–24.

Guerra, C. Cardoso. (2015). La poética adivinatoria de Ifa: Transculturación yòrùbà en la escritura caribeña. PhD dissertation, Universidad de Las Palmas de Gran Canaria.

Halloy, A. (2012). Gods in the flesh: Learning emotions in the Xangô possession cult (Brazil). *Ethnos*, 77(2), 177–202. https://doi.org/10.1080/00141844.2011.586465.

Harding, R. E. (2006). É a Senzala: Slavery, women, and embodied knowledge in Afro-Brazilian Candomblé. In R. M. Griffith and B. D. Savage, eds., *Women and Religion in the African Diaspora: Knowledge, Power, and Performance*. Baltimore, MD: Johns Hopkins University Press, pp. 3–18.

Harvey, S. A. (2013). "Big Apple Vodou." *Narratively*, March 6. https://narratively.com/big-apple-vodou.

Healy, M. S. (1998). Empire, race and war: Black participation in British military efforts during the twentieth century. PhD dissertation, Loyola University Chicago.

Hebblethwaite, B. (2012). *Vodou Songs in Haitian Creole and English*. Philadelphia, PA: Temple University Press.

Hegel, G. W. F. ([1837] 2001). *The Philosophy of History*, trans. J. Sibree. Ontario: Batoche.

Herskovits, M. J., and Herskovits, F. S. (1934). *Rebel Destiny: Among the Bush Negros of Dutch Guiana*. New York: Whittlesey House, McGraw-Hill.

Hoffman, S. J. (1992). Sport, religion, and ethics. In S. J. Hoffman, ed., *Sport and Religion*. Champaign, IL: Human Kinetics, pp. 213–26.

Holbraad, M. (2008). Definitive evidence, from Cuban gods. *Journal of the Royal Anthropological Institute*, 14(s1), S93–S109.

(2012). *Truth in Motion: The Recursive Anthropology of Cuban Divination*. Chicago, IL: University of Chicago Press.

hooks, b. (2000). *Feminist Theory: From Margin to Center*. London: Pluto Press.

Hornback, R. (2019). *Racism and Early Blackface Comic Traditions: From the Old World to the New*. New York: Palgrave Macmillan.

Houk, J. T. (1995). *Spirits, Blood, and Drums: The Orisha Religion in Trinidad*. Philadelphia, PA: Temple University Press.

Huet, N. B. Juárez. (2013). Transnational networks and re-Africanization of the Santería in Mexico City. In E. Cunin and O. Hoffmann, eds., *Blackness and Mestizaje in Mexico and Central America*. Trenton, NJ: AfricaWorld Press, pp.165–90.

Johnson, P. C. (2002). Models of "the body" in the ethnographic field: Garifuna and Candomblé case studies. *Method and Theory in the Study of Religion*, 14(2), 170–95.

(2011). An Atlantic genealogy of spirit possession. *Comparative Studies in Society and History*, 53(2), 393–425.

Knipe, D. M. (2015). *Vedic Voices: Intimate Narratives of a Living Andhra Tradition*. New York: Oxford University Press.

Lara, A.-M. (2020). *Queer Freedom : Black Sovereignty*. Albany: State University of New York Press.

Lawal, B. (2008). Èjìwàpò: The dialectics of twoness in Yorùbá art and culture. *African Arts*, 41(1), 24–39.

LeBlanc, R. M. (2010). *The Art of the Gut: Manhood, Power, and Ethics in Japanese Politics*. Berkeley: University of California Press.

Lele, O. (2001). *Obí: Oracle of Cuban Santería*. Rochester, VT: Destiny.

(2003). *The Diloggún: The Orishas, Proverbs, Sacrifices, and Prohibitions of Cuban Santería*. Rochester, VT: Destiny.

(2012). *Sacrificial Ceremonies of Santería: A Complete Guide to the Rituals and Practices*. Rochester, VT: Destiny.

Le Reste, J.-Y., Coppens, M., and Barais, M., et al. (2013). The transculturality of "gut feelings": Results from a French Delphi consensus survey. *European Journal of General Practice*, 19(4), 237–24.

Lessa, L. Falcão. (2019). Nossos Passos Vêm de Longe: A Irmandade da Boa Morte de São Gonçalo Dos Campos à Luz do Feminismo

Negro. *ENECULT: Encontro de Estudos Multidisciplinares em Cultura*, August. www.xvenecult.ufba.br/modulos/submissao/Upload-484/ 111445.pdf (unpaginated).

Lesshafft, H. (2016). Circles of care: Healing practices in a Bahian Candomblé community. PhD dissertation, University of Edinburgh.

Li, X. (2007). *Voices Rising: Asian Canadian Cultural Activism*. Vancouver: University of British Columbia Press.

Liyanage, S. (2016). "Bokken ranga pāmuda": Gut feeling, instinct and rhetoric of Sri Lankan actor learning. *Journal of Aesthetic and Fine Arts*, 1(1), 22–33.

Lloyd, D., and Wolfe. P. (2015). Settler colonial logics and the neoliberal regime. *Settler Colonial Studies*, 6(2): 1–10.

Lohmann, R. I. (2003). Turning the belly: Insights on religious conversion from New Guinea gut feelings. In A. Buckser and S. D. Glazier, eds., *The Anthropology of Religious Conversion*. New York: Rowman and Littlefield, pp. 109–21.

(2011). Empathetic perception and imagination among the Asabano: Lessons for anthropology. In D. W. Holland and C. J. Troop, eds., *The Anthropology of Empathy: Experiencing the Lives of Others in Pacific Societies*. New York: Berghahn, pp. 95–116.

Lucas, G. (2018). Gut thinking: The gut microbiome and mental health beyond the head. *Microbial Ecology in Health and Disease*, 29(2), 1548250. https://doi.org/10.1080/16512235.2018.1548250.

Luhrmann, T. M. (2014). Response: Knowing God, attentional learning, and the local theory of mind. *Religion, Brain & Behavior*, 4(1), 78–90.

MacGaffey, W., Harris, M. D., Williams, S. H., and Driskell, D.C. (1993). *Astonishment & Power: The Eyes of Understanding: Kongo Minkisi / The Art of Renée Stout*. Washington, DC: Smithsonian Institution.

Machon, J. (2009). *(Syn)Aesthetics: Redefining Visceral Performance*. New York: Palgrave Macmillan.

Madan, M. ([2005] 2021). *Pocket Manual for Santeros*. Caracas: Ediciones Òrúnmìlà.

Maffi, L. (1994). A linguistic analysis of Tzeltal Maya ethnosymptomatology. PhD dissertation, University of California–Berkeley.

Marchal, J. A. (2019). The disgusting apostle and a queer affect between epistles and audiences. In F. C. Black and J. L. Koosed, eds., *Reading with Feeling: Affect Theory and the Bible*. Atlanta, GA: SBL Press, pp. 113–40.

Martín, F. Ferrándiz, and Rodero, C. G. (2005). Espejos: Cuerpos, imágenes y palabras en el culto de María Lionza. In C. Ortiz García, C. Sánchez Carretero, and A. Cea Gutiérrez, eds., *Maneras de mirar: lecturas antropológicas de la fotografía*. Madrid: CSIC, pp. 257–79.

Mason, J. (1992). *Orin Òrìṣà: Songs for Selected Heads*. Brooklyn, NY: Yoruba Theological Archministry.

(1997). Ogun: Builder of the Lukumi's house. In S. T. Barnes, ed., *Africa's Ogun: Old World and New*. Bloomington: Indiana University Press, pp. 353–68.

(1999). *Ìdáná Fún Òrìṣà: Cooking for Selected Heads*. Brooklyn, NY: Yoruba Theological Archministry.

Matibag, E. (1996). *Afro-Cuban Religious Experience: Cultural Reflections in Narrative*. Gainesville: University Press of Florida.

Matory, J. L. (1994). *Sex and the Empire That Is No More: Gender and the Politics of Metaphor in Oyo Yoruba Religion*. Minneapolis: University of Minnesota Press.

(2005). *Black Atlantic Religion: Tradition, Transnationalism, and Matriarchy in the Afro-Brazilian Candomblé*. Princeton, NJ: Princeton University Press.

(2018). *The Fetish Revisited: Marx, Freud, and the Gods Black People Make*. Durham, NC: Duke University Press.

Mattos, H. (2008). "Black troops" and hierarchies of color in the Portuguese Atlantic world: The case of Henrique Dias and his Black regiment. *Luso-Brazilian Review*, 45(1), 6–29.

Mazzarella, W. (2009). Affect: What is it good for? In S. Dube, ed., *Enchantments of Modernity: Empire, Nation, Globalization*. New York: Routledge/Taylor & Francis, pp. 291–309.

Mbembe, A. (2003). Necropolitics. *Public Culture*, 15(1),11–40.

Medina, T. Pérez, and Herrera Hernández, E. (1995). *El camino de Osha: ceremonias, ritos, y secretos*. Caracas: Editorial Panapo.

Méndez, E. Fernández. ([1964] 1970). *Historia de la cultura en Puerto Rico, 1493–1960*. San Juan: Ediciones "El Cemí."

Menéndez, L., ed. (1998). Libreta de Santería de Jesús Torregrosa. In *Estudios Afro-Cubanos: Selección de lecturas*, vol. 3. Havana: Universidad de La Habana, pp. 17–268.

Métraux, A. (1959). *Voodoo in Haiti*, trans. H. Charteris. New York: Oxford University Press.

Miletti-González, E. M. (2013). Palo Monte. In P. Taylor and F. I. Case, eds., *The Encyclopedia of Caribbean Religions: Volume 2, M–Z*. Urbana: University of Illinois Press, pp. 661–9.

Mintz, S. W., and Price, R. ([1976] 1992). *The Birth of African-American Culture: An Anthropological Perspective*. Rev. ed. Boston, MA: Beacon.

Modern, J. L. (2021). *Neuromatic: Or, A Particular History of Religion and the Brain*. Chicago, IL: University of Chicago Press.

Moliner, I. (2013). Arará. In P. Taylor and F. I., eds. *The Encyclopedia of Caribbean Religions: Volume 1, A–L*. Urbana: University of Illinois Press, pp.70–7.

Morison, R. (1906). Remarks on some functions of the omentum. *British Medical Journal*, 1(2350), 76–8.

Motta, R. (2005). Body trance and word trance in Brazilian religion. *Current Sociology*, 53(2), 293–308.

Murphy, J. (1993). *Santería: An African Religion in America*. Boston, MA: Beacon Press.

Neto, N. A. L., Brooks, S. E., and Alves, R. R. N. (2009). From Eshu to Obatala: Animals used in sacrificial rituals at Candomblé "terreiros" in Brazil. *Journal of Ethnobiology and Ethnomedicine*, 5(23), 1–10.

Nzengou-Tayo, M. J. (2007). Haitian callaloo: What you ask for is certainly not what you get! *Callaloo*, 30(1), 175–8.

Ó Tuathail, G. (2003). "Just out looking for a fight": American affect and the invasion of Iraq. *Antipode*, 35(5), 856–70.

Ochoa, T. R. (2005). Aspects of the dead. In M. A. Font, ed., *Cuba Today: Continuity and Change since the "Periodo Especial."* New York: Bildner Center for Western Hemisphere Studies, CUNY Graduate Center, pp. 245–60.

(2007). Versions of the dead: Kalunga, Cuban-Kongo materiality, and ethnography. *Cultural Anthropology*, 22(4), 473–500.

(2010). *Society of the Dead: Quita Manaquita and Palo Praise in Cuba*. Berkeley: University of California Press.

de Oliveira Pereira, A. C. (2015). Mulheres, género, resistência e autoridade em e através do Candomblé de Salvador, Bahia; Womanhood, Gender, Resistance and Authority in and through Candomblé of Salvador, Bahia. BA thesis, Brandeis University.

Omi olo Oshun, O. T. A. (2009). *Oddun of Ita or Consulta for the Diviner: Okana Sorde (1) Where the World Began with One, to Obara (6) A King Should Not Lie*. Raleigh, NC: Lulu Press.

Onians, R. B. (1951). *The Origins of European Thought about the Body, the Mind, the Soul, the World, Time, and Fate*. Cambridge: Cambridge University Press.

Ortiz, F. (1923). *Un catauro de cubanismos: Apuntes lexicograficos*. Havana: publisher unspecified.

Owomoyela, O. (2008). *Yoruba Proverbs*. Lincoln: University of Nebraska Press.

Palmié, S. (2013). *The Cooking of History: How Not to Study Afro-Cuban Religion*. Chicago, IL: University of Chicago Press.

(2018). When is a thing? Transduction and immediacy in Afro-Cuban ritual; or, ANT in Matanzas, Cuba, summer of 1948. *Comparative Studies in Society and History*, 60(4), 786–809.

Paton, D. (2009). Obeah acts: Producing and policing the boundaries of religion in the Caribbean. *Small Axe*, 13(1), 1–18.

Payne-Jackson, A., and Alleyne, M. C. (2004). *Jamaican Folk Medicine: A Source of Healing*. Kingston: University of the West Indies Press.

Pérez, E. (2013a). Willful spirits and weakened flesh: Historicizing the initiation narrative in Afro-Cuban religions. *Journal of Africana Religions*, 1(2), 151–93.

(2013b). Portable portals: Transnational rituals for the head across globalizing orisha traditions. *Nova Religio*, 16(4), 35–62.

(2016). *Religion in the Kitchen: Cooking, Talking, and the Making of Black Atlantic Traditions*. New York: New York University Press.

(2021). Hail to the chefs: Black women's pedagogy, kitchenspaces, and Afro-Diasporic religions. In J. Hobson, ed., *The Routledge Companion to Black Women's Cultural Histories: Across the Diaspora, from Ancient Times to the Present*. New York: Routledge, pp. 333–41.

Pietz, W. (1988). The problem of the fetish, IIIa. *Res*, 16, 105–23.

Platvoet, J. G. (1982). *Comparing Religions: A Limitative Approach: An Analysis of Akan, ParaCreole, and IFO-Sananda Rites and Prayers*. The Hague: Mouton.

Povinelli, E. (2006). *The Empire of Love: Toward a Theory of Intimacy, Genealogy, and Carnality*. Durham, NC: Duke University Press.

Price, R. (2007). *Travels with Tooy: History, Memory, and the African American Imagination*. Chicago, IL: University of Chicago Press.

Prince, A. (2001). How shall we sing the Lord's song in a strange land? Constructing the divine in Caribbean contexts. In P. Taylor, ed., *Nation Dance: Religion, Identity and Cultural Difference in the Caribbean*. Bloomington: Indiana University Press, pp. 25–31.

Prinz, J. J. (2004). *Gut Reactions: A Perceptual Theory of Emotion*. Oxford: Oxford University Press.

Rabelais, F. (1854). *Oeuvres de François Rabelais contenant la vie de Gargantua et celle de Pantagruel*. Paris: J. Bry Ainé.

Ramos, M. W. (2011). *Orí Eledá mí ó . . . Si mi cabeza no me vende*. Miami, FL: Eleda.org.

(2012). *Obí Agbón: Lukumí Divination with Coconut*. Miami, FL: Eleda.org.

(2013). Lucumí (Yoruba) culture in Cuba: A reevaluation (1830s–1940s). PhD dissertation, Florida International University.

Rey, T., and Richman, K. (2010). The somatics of syncretism: Tying body and soul in Haitian religion. *Studies in Religion/Sciences religieuses*, 39(3), 379–403.

Richman, K. E. (2005). *Migration and Vodou*. Gainesville: University Press of Florida.

Robinson, D. (2013). *Displacement and the Somatics of Postcolonial Culture*. Columbus: Ohio State University.

Romberg, R. (2003). *Witchcraft and Welfare: Spiritual Capital and the Business of Magic in Modern Puerto*. Austin: University of Texas Press.

(2007). "Today, Changó is Changó": How Africanness becomes a ritual commodity in Puerto Rico. *Western Folklore*, 66(½), 75–106.

Roumain, J. ([1944] 2000). *Gouverneurs de la rosée*. Paris: Temps des cerises.

Sager, R. D. (2009). My song is my bond: Haitian Vodou singing and the transformation of being. *The World of Music*, 51(2), 91–118.

Sánchez, J. (1978). *La religión de los orichas: creencias y ceremonias de un culto afro-caribeño*. San Juan: Ramallo Bros.

(2004). *Los Alagbas*. Unpublished manuscript.

Sánchez Cervera, A. (2022). "¿De qué nos previenen las dos letras del año 2022 en Cuba?" *Afrocubanas: La revista*, January 22. https://bit.ly/3Tym04J.

Schwarcz, L. M. (2003). Not black, not white: Just the opposite. Culture, race and national identity in Brazil. Centre for Brazilian Studies, University of Oxford, unpublished Working Paper CBS-47–03. www.lac.ox.ac.uk/sites/default/files/lac/documents/media/schwarcz47.pdf.

Schaffler, Y., and Brabec de Mori, B. (2017). *Cuando el misterio insiste:* The construction of authority in Dominican Vodou. *International Forum on Audio-Visual Research/Jahrbuch des Phonogrammarchivs*, 7, 138–66.

Scott, D. (1997). An obscure miracle of connection: Discursive tradition and black diaspora criticism. *Small Axe*, 1: 17–36.

da Silva, R. Nascimento. (2018). A máscara obscura do ódio racial: Segregação, anonimato e violência nas redes sociais. MA thesis, Universidade Federal Fluminense.

da Silva Paim, M. R. (2005). Do Sete à São Joaquim: O cotidiano de mulheres de saia e homens feirantes em feiras soteropolitanas 1964–73. MA thesis, Federal University of Bahia.

Smidt, W. (2004). Fetishists and magicians: The description of African religions by Immanuel Kant (1724–1804). In F. Ludwig and A. Adogame, eds., *European Traditions in the Study of Religion in Africa*. Wiesbaden: Harrasowitz, pp. 109–16.

Smith, J. Z. (1990). *Drudgery Divine*. Chicago, IL: University of Chicago Press.

Sobo, E. J. (1993). *One Blood: The Jamaican Body*. Albany: State University of New York Press.

Soyinka, W. (2002). *Salutations to the Gut*. Ibadan: Bookcraft Ltd, Pocket Gifts.

Stevens, A. M. (1995). Manje in Haitian culture: The symbolic significance of manje in Haitian culture. *Journal of Haitian Studies*, 1(1), 75–88.

Stroeken, K. (2008). Sensory shifts and "synaesthetics" in Sukuma healing. *Ethnos*, 73(4), 466–84.

Strongman, R. (2013). The body of Vodou: Corporeality and the location of gender in Afro-Diasporic religion. In C. P. Marsh-Lockett and E. J. West, eds., *Literary Expressions of African Spirituality*. Lanham, MD: Lexington, pp. 99–118.

Stannard, R. (1982). *Science and the Renewal of Belief*. London: SCM Press.

Stephen, H. J. M. (1985). *Winti: Afro-Surinaamse religie en magische rituelen in Suriname en Nederland*. Amsterdam: Karnak.

Swartz, M. H. (2010). *Tratado de semiología: anamnesis y exploración*. Madrid: Elsevier España.

Targète, J., and Urciolo, R. G., eds. (1993). *Haitian Creole–English Dictionary*. Chantilly, VA: Dunwoody Press.

Taves, A. (2014). Cognitive science, learning, and "theory of mind." *The Religious Studies Project*, December 5. www.religiousstudiesproject.com/response/cognitive-science-learning-and-theory-of-mind-by-ann-taves.

Thite, G. U. (1970). Animal-sacrifice in the Brāhmaṇatexts. *Numen*, 17(2), 143–58.

Thoden van Velzen, H. U. E., and van Wetering, W. (2004). *In the Shadow of the Oracle: Religion As Politics in a Suriname Maroon Society*. Long Grove, IL: Waveland Press.

Thomas, K. (1971). *Religion and the Decline of Magic: Studies in Popular Beliefs in Sixteenth and Seventeenth-Century England*. London: Weidenfeld and Nicolson.

Thompson, R. F. (1983). *Flash of the Spirit: African & Afro-American Art & Philosophy*. New York: Random House.

Thornton, B. (2021). Refiguring Christianity and Black Atlantic religion: Representation, essentialism, and Christian variation in the southern Caribbean. *Journal of the American Academy of Religion*, 89(1), 41–71.

Trouillot, M.-R. (1995). *Silencing the Past: Power and the Production of History*. Boston, MA: Beacon Press.

(2021). *Stirring the Pot of Haitian History*, trans. B. Hebblethwaite and M. F. Past. Liverpool: Liverpool University Press.

Tudela, J. A. G., O'Connor Ramos, Y., and Guevara Labaut, A. (2013). De la cooperación ritual a la multirreligiosidad: Las conexiones cubano-haitianas en el Complejo Ritual de Lajas (Contramaestre, Cuba). *Batey: Revista Cubana de Antropología Sociocultural*, 4(4), 33–55.

Turner, K. (2021). Deep folklore/queer folkloristics. In J. A. Fivecoate, K. Downs, and M. A. E. McGriff, eds., *Advancing Folkloristics*. Bloomington: Indiana University Press, pp. 9–34.

Turner, V. (1978). Encounter with Freud: The making of a comparative symbologist. In G. D. Spindler, ed., *The Making of Psychological Anthropology*. Berkeley: University of California Press, pp. 558–82.

Viladrich, A. (2009). Between bellyaches and lucky charms: Revealing Latinos' plant-healing knowledge and practices in New York City. In A. Pieroni and I. Vandebroek, eds., *Traveling Cultures and Plants: The Ethnobiology and Ethnopharmacy of Human Migrations*. New York: Berghahn, pp.64–85.

Viveiros de Castro, E. (2009). GUT feelings about Amazonia: Potential affinity and the construction of sociality. In L. M. Rival and N. L. Whitehead, eds., *Beyond the Visible and the Material: The Amerindianization of Society in the Work of Peter Rivière*. Oxford: Oxford University Press, pp.19–43.

von Gleich, P. (2015). African American narratives of captivity and fugitivity: Developing post-slavery questions for *Angela Davis: An Autobiography*. *COPAS: Current Objectives of Postgraduate American Studies*, 16(1), 1–18.

von Poser, A. (2013). *Foodways and Empathy: Relatedness in a Ramu River Society, Papua New Guinea*. New York: Berghahn.

Warnier, J.-P. (2007). *The Pot-King: The Body and Technologies of Power*. Leyden: Brill.

Wehmeyer, S. C. (2000). Indian altars of the spiritual church: Kongo echoes in New Orleans. *African Arts*, 33(4), 62–70, 95–6.

Wekker, G. (2006). *The Politics of Passion: Women's Sexual Culture in the Afro-Surinamese Diaspora*. New York: Columbia University Press.

Willerslev, R. (2007). *Soul Hunters: Hunting, Animism, and Personhood among the Siberian Yukaghirs*. Berkeley: University of California Press.

Winterson, J. (1997). *Gut Symmetries*. New York: Alfred A. Knopf.

Wiredu, K. (2004). Identity as an intellectual problem. In J. I. Cabezón and S. G. Davaney, eds., *Identity and the Politics of Scholarship in the Study of Religion*. New York: Routledge, pp. 209–28.

Wisneski, D. C., Lytle, B. L., and Skitka, L. J. 2009. Gut reactions: Moral conviction, religiosity, and trust in authority. *Psychological Science*, 20, 1059–63.

Wooding, C. J. (1981). *Evolving Culture: A Cross-cultural Study of Suriname, West Africa, and the Caribbean.* Washington, DC: University Press of America.

Wynn, M. R. (2005). *Emotional Experience and Religious Understanding: Integrating Perception, Conception and Feeling.* Cambridge: Cambridge University Press.

# Acknowledgments

Like Elegguá, Ashabi Mosely, Arlene Stevens, and the members of Ilé Laroye should be acknowledged first.[1] Thank you.

My thinking about gut feelings reached a turning point when I was invited by Todne Thomas and Fred Klaits to join a panel on "Social Death and Vital Relations in African American Religions" at the November 2018 American Anthropological Association Annual Meeting. I would like to thank them and Aisha Beliso-De Jesús, N. Fadeke Castor, and Onaje X. O. Woodbine for that conversation. Different aspects of my argument were subsequently developed at the Religious Studies reading group at the University of North Carolina at Chapel Hill in January 2019, Princeton University's "Religions of the Americas" workshop in March 2019, and "Gastro-Politics and Gastro-Ethics of the Sacred & the Secular in Contemporary Plural Societies," a conference convened by the Max Planck Institute for the Study of Religious & Ethnic Diversity and the Meertens Institute, Amsterdam, in November 2019. Among those to whom I am most grateful are Lauren Leve, Brendan Thornton, Brandon Bayne, Juliane Hammer, and Alejandro Stephano Escalante at UNC-Chapel Hill; Wallace D. Best, Judith Weisenfeld, Seth A. Perry, Kijan A. Bloomfield, Eziaku Nwokocha, Andrew Walker-Cornetta, Nyle E. Fort, Ahmad Greene-Hayes, and Lynn Davidman at Princeton; and Annalisa Butticci, Birgit Meyer, Peter van der Veer, and Irene Stengs. *Un agradecimiento especial* is owed to Jessica Delgado.

My thanks also go out to Marion Gibson, as editor of the Cambridge Elements in Magic; Alex Wright, at Cambridge University Press; Stephan Palmié, for the generative introduction to Antoni Miralda, and Sr. Miralda himself; and my supportive colleagues at the University of California, Santa Barbara, including Fabio Rambelli and Kathleen M. Moore. My mother, Ivonne Pérez, made so many things possible. Raphael and Georgina gave those things meaning beyond measure.

---

[1] As in my previous publications, these are pseudonyms.

*For Wm.*

Cambridge Elements ≡

# Magic

## Marion Gibson
*University of Exeter*

Marion Gibson is Professor of Renaissance and Magical Literatures and Director of the Flexible Combined Honours Programme at the University of Exeter. Her publications include *Possession, Puritanism and Print: Darrell, Harsnett, Shakespeare and the Elizabethan Exorcism Controversy* (2006), *Witchcraft Myths in American Culture* (2007), *Imagining the Pagan Past: Gods and Goddesses in Literature and History since the Dark Ages* (2013), *The Arden Shakespeare Dictionary of Shakespeare's Demonology* (with Jo Esra, 2014), *Rediscovering Renaissance Witchcraft* (2017) and *Witchcraft: The Basics* (2018). Her new book, *The Witches of St Osyth: Persecution, Murder and Betrayal in Elizabethan England*, will be published by CUP in 2022.

## About the Series

Elements in Magic aims to restore the study of magic, broadly defined, to a central place within culture: one which it occupied for many centuries before being set apart by changing discourses of rationality and meaning. Understood as a continuing and potent force within global civilisation, magical thinking is imaginatively approached here as a cluster of activities, attitudes, beliefs and motivations which include topics such as alchemy, astrology, divination, exorcism, the fantastical, folklore, haunting, supernatural creatures, necromancy, ritual, spirit possession and witchcraft.

**Cambridge Elements** ☰

# Magic

---

## Elements in the Series

Printed in the United States
by Baker & Taylor Publisher Services